RELEASING
YOUR
Children
TO THE
LORD

RELEASING
YOUR
Children
TO THE
LORD

A STORY
& GUIDE FOR
PARENTS

Gunila Baumann
WITH JEMIMAH WRIGHT

YWAM PUBLISHING
Seattle, Washington

YWAM Publishing is the publishing ministry of Youth With A Mission (YWAM), an international missionary organization of Christians from many denominations dedicated to presenting Jesus Christ to this generation. To this end, YWAM has focused its efforts in three main areas: (1) training and equipping believers for their part in fulfilling the Great Commission (Matthew 28:19), (2) personal evangelism, and (3) mercy ministry (medical and relief work).

For a free catalog of books and materials, call (425) 771-1153 or (800) 922-2143. Visit us online at www.ywampublishing.com.

This title is available as an e-book. Visit www.ywampublishing.com.

Library of Congress Cataloging-in-Publication Data
Baumann, Gunila.
    Releasing your children to the Lord : a story and guide for parents /
Gunila Baumann with Jemimah Wright ; foreword by Floyd and Sally McClung.
        p. cm.
    ISBN 978-1-57658-554-2
    1. Baumann, Gunila. 2. Youth with a Mission, Inc. 3. Missionaries—Family relationships. 4. Parent and child—Religious aspects—Christianity. I. Wright, Jemimah. II. Title.
    BV2360.Y74B38 2012
    266.0092'2—dc23
    [B]   2011040199

Some names have been changed in the stories throughout this book to protect the privacy of individuals.

First printing 2012

Printed in the United States of America

To my three children,
Elisabeth, Dan, and Christina,
without whom this book could not have been written

Contents

Foreword

When a mother and father invest everything in their children, they literally put their lives on the line for them. They stake their future, their finances, their reputation—everything. No parent claims to be perfect, but what good parents do commit to is giving their lives away for their children. They are acting on the biblical principle that those who give up their lives will find them.

Hans and Gunila found their lives in their children, many times over, not just physically, but spiritually as well. They gave their lives away for their two daughters and son and found that God gave back to them three world-changers who dared to go to the ends of the earth for Jesus.

Every child with spiritual ambition is a test to their mother and father. We mean it as parents when we dedicate them to the Lord as little ones, but do any of us actually think or dream in our wildest imagination that they will go to prison for their faith? Or be arrested for spreading the gospel? Or choose to live among religious extremists in one of the most complex and remote urban centers in the world?

This is an honest book—you will find help for your own struggle and passion to be a good mother and father to your children. As parents we need reassurance along the way, comfort and wise words to help us fulfill our responsibility to our kids.

Sally and I have been impacted by Gunila and how she prays for her children. We will never forget the moment when we were praying together in one of our community gatherings for her son, Dan, in prison in Iran. With tears streaming down her cheeks, she exclaimed to God, "Father, don't let Dan out of prison until all of your purposes are accomplished in his being there. Give him courage and protect him, Father, but most of all I pray that you will use him for your glory . . ."

I'll never forget the look on Dan's face when I told him several years later how his mother prayed for him while he was imprisoned in Iran! Of course, he knew by then that his mother and father had surrendered him and his sisters to the Lord. But it was quite amazing to him to be reminded that his mom was more concerned with him obeying God than being set free from prison. Oh, for more mothers with a heart like that!

One of the most compelling things about this story is how much Hans and Gunila are like the rest of us. They were not flashy, boisterous parents. What set them apart was the courage and faith they demonstrated when it came to their children. They consciously let their children go.

You can do the same. Their story will give you the courage you need to do the same for your children. Their example will impart faith to you. And the truths they lived by will guide you to raise your children to be world-changers. Far better to let them go and to see them serve God than to hang on to them but see them live lukewarm, wishy-washy Christian lives as a result.

A mom once begged me to talk to her daughter about the Lord. "Please, Floyd, can't you tell her to serve God? Please, do something . . . she has strayed so far from the Lord!" As I asked questions, this broken-hearted mother confessed that when her teenage daughter had first expressed interest in going on short-term outreaches and serving God as a missionary, she had thrown a wet blanket on her enthusiasm. She had done everything she could to hold on to daughter, only to lose her in the end to the world.

Mom and dad: the most important decision you will make in life besides loving Jesus and marrying each other is to dedicate your children to God. Perhaps you already did that when they were infants. Don't take them back! And don't only leave them in God's hands; do all you can to disciple them and encourage them to serve God with their whole heart.

Releasing Your Children to the Lord will help guide you and encourage you to let your children go. At the end of each chapter there are a set of "Principles to Live By"—they alone are worth the price of this book.

We encourage every mother and father we know to read this jaw-dropping, heart-touching story of God at work in the lives of three of the most amazing "children" you will ever read about. Lis, Dan, and Christina are all friends of our family. We are inspired by their lives and are thankful such an amazing story has now been put in writing for the world to read.

May it inspire you to do the same with your children and grandchildren!

Floyd and Sally McClung
All Nations
Cape Town, South Africa

1

IN GOD'S HANDS

Ask of me, and I will make the nations your
inheritance, the ends of the earth your possession.
—Psalm 2:8

Walking into the plush hotel lobby, I was filled with excitement at what was to come. I had been looking forward to this Lydia Prayer Conference in Washington, DC, for months. The year was 1985, and it was my first visit to this city, far away from my home and family in Southern California.

Silently I thanked the Lord for his goodness in bringing me here, and his faithfulness to our family. My husband Hans's job in construction was going well, and our three children were all happy and in good health.

"Gunila, hello!" came a voice behind me, bringing me back to the present.

"Hello," I replied, smiling at my pastor's wife, Shirley Wacker. Shirley and another woman from our church, Peg

Bevens, had arrived on a different plane. We would all be sharing a room in the hotel, and I was so pleased to see them.

"Let's register and get something to eat," Shirley said with a smile.

We went up to the room, and as we entered, the phone started ringing. It was a woman from reception calling for me. They had a message from Hans asking me to call home.

"I hope nothing has happened," I said, trying to ignore thoughts of accidents or other such horrors.

Quickly I picked up the phone and dialed home. There was a three-hour time difference, so I didn't know if Hans would be in.

"Hello, Hans Baumann speaking."

"Hans, I got a message to call you. Is everything alright?" I asked.

"I think you may need to sit down," he said.

He went on to tell me that the US State Department had contacted him to let us know that our oldest daughter, Elisabeth, had been imprisoned in Nepal one week earlier. She was facing a sentence of up to three years on charges of converting Nepalis to Christianity.

Elisabeth, or Lis for short, was our firstborn. She was bold and adventurous. Now only twenty-three years old, she had served as a missionary in Nepal for nearly three years with Youth With A Mission (YWAM). Hans told me that Lis had been trekking in the mountains with a team of fourteen people. They were going to meet some new believers in a village on an invitation from a local pastor. As they were leaving the village, they were arrested. Nepal, a primarily Hindu country, had a law that if you were caught changing religion or converting someone to another religion, you could be sentenced to several years in prison. Many Christians were languishing in cells because of their faith.

I knew there was nothing else I could do but pray, so I said good-bye to Hans and joined Shirley and the others. We sat together in a little coffee shop and quietly lifted up my daughter and her team to the Lord, asking for his protection and favor on their lives. Later I realized I was in the best place possible, when Shirley told Shelagh McAlpine, the leader of Lydia, what had happened. Shelagh got the whole conference—over three hundred women—praying for Lis and the team.

When Lis first told us she felt God calling her to Nepal, I knew that it wouldn't always be easy or safe. This was the first time something very serious had happened, and I couldn't be close at hand to help my daughter. Now more than ever, I had to trust her to God's hands. As I kept on giving Elisabeth back to the Lord, I felt God's presence with me. We sang the words of one worship song many times: "Ascribe greatness to our God, the Rock; his work is perfect and all his ways are just," taken from Deuteronomy 32:3–4. Each time, I agreed with the words in my heart, and I was filled with confidence that Elisabeth was in God's care. He who is faithful and just in all his ways was watching over her.

The next day I was in a seminar when someone arrived with word of an urgent call for me. Panic gripped me. I could feel my heart thumping in my chest as worried thoughts ran through my mind. Flustered, I picked up my things and raced out of the room, dreading the news I was going to receive.

"Hello," I said cautiously as I picked up the phone.

This time it was the US State Department. Lis was okay, although still in prison. The consulate was doing all it could to secure her release. I breathed a sigh of relief that nothing worse had happened to our daughter.

Because the whole conference knew of my situation, women were coming up to me asking if there was any news and telling me they were praying. It really helped, and I was so touched by their concern.

On the third day I received another call. "Elisabeth has been released on bail," Hans said joyfully. For an instant I was speechless. She had been in prison for nine days. I knew it was a miracle that she was released, but I only found out later how much of a miracle it was.

The next morning I was asked to address the conference and tell everyone the good news. I walked up to the platform and hugged Shelagh. I was close to tears as I announced that my daughter was free. The crowd of women cheered and clapped when they heard Lis had been released; it was such an immediate answer to all our prayers. I quoted the song that had touched me, "Ascribe Greatness," speaking it out as a praise to the God who so faithfully looks after us.

Later that night I tried several times to phone Lis but couldn't get through. After midnight I decided to give up.

"Try one more time," Shirley urged.

"Okay," I said, holding little hope that I would get through.

"Hello?" came the voice at the other end of the line, thousands of miles away from the comfort of my hotel room.

"Elisabeth, is that you?" I exclaimed, amazed that I was actually speaking to my daughter.

She said she was safe and well and gave me a rundown of what had happened. Her team of nine foreigners and five Nepali carriers had hiked for five days high into the mountains to visit new Christians in a small village. The team was full of excitement to meet new believers, who had invited them to come and teach about Jesus. The team had devised a way of sharing stories from the Bible through puppet shows and drama so that everyone could understand the message. They enjoyed their time with the villagers and made many new friends.

But unknown to the team, the local Buddhist priest was angry at their being there. He was upset with the villagers who had become Christians, as it meant he was losing his power and influence over the people. The priest contacted authorities and told them about Elisabeth and the others, saying they were converting the village to Christianity and had even killed a cow (not true, of course), which was an automatic six-year jail sentence.

As the group was preparing to leave the village, they were accosted by two policemen who asked for their papers. The police said there was something wrong with their visas, and everyone was arrested and taken to detention. The team then had to trek another two days with the policemen to get to the nearest village with a jail and courthouse. They knew then that this was about more than just their papers.

They were not handcuffed, simply told to sit outside the jail and wait. The group was exhausted and confused at what their crime was. All they could do was sit and listen to the policemen heatedly discuss their fate. Lis noticed that the guards didn't seem interested in the Nepali carriers, only the Western prisoners. The team realized it might be possible for a carrier to escape. They decided the best person for the job was a Nepali man named Prem, who was in his forties and very loyal. Prem came from the mountains and had led a simple life, but now he was the team's hope in getting word out that they needed help.

Prem's escape began with a toilet break. To go to the toilet, team members were led two by two into the bushes, but the guards didn't stay to watch them. So the team gave Prem a piece of paper with the name and address of the YWAM team in Kathmandu and said to tell them about the situation. This would be no simple feat. Prem had rarely used public transport and had been in Kathmandu only once before. He was very fearful but wanted to help his friends.

One of the team members called to the guards that he and Prem needed to go to the toilet. Lazily, a guard got off his stool. He led the two into the bushes behind the jail and then went back to his stool. This was Prem's chance. Without looking back, he made a run for freedom. After a few minutes, the team member walked back to the group.

A little while later, one guard looked around. "Are you missing someone?" he asked. The team stayed silent. The guard shrugged his shoulders and moved on.

Prem's escape was a success, but there was a problem. At first he stayed in the village, not knowing how to get to Kathmandu, a six-hour drive away. To make matters worse, he had been given the wrong piece of paper. He didn't have the contact details he needed and had no idea how to get hold of the YWAM team in Kathmandu.

By this time the whole team was moved into a tiny cell. It was so small they could only sleep side by side like sardines, with no room to turn over. Quietly, they prayed in the dark cell, asking God to help them.

The next day the police took the team to court to be tried and to sign papers admitting to the offenses. On the way they had to walk handcuffed along the street. As they were walking, they spotted Prem. One of the team subtly tried to urge him to get help, without drawing the attention of the guards. They were very discouraged to see that he was still in the village and hadn't left for Kathmandu. It seemed like help would never come.

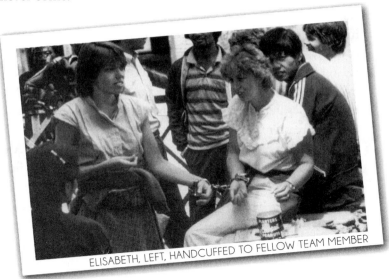

ELISABETH, LEFT, HANDCUFFED TO FELLOW TEAM MEMBER

At the court the team asked for a lawyer. They were provided with one, and they told him everything, only to find out he was on the side of the police and wasn't going to help. It looked like they were stuck in a corner. They wouldn't be released until they signed the papers, but if they signed, they would be sentenced to at least three years.

Meanwhile, Prem finally made his way to Kathmandu, but without directions he had no idea where to go. For three days he wandered the streets, wondering how he was going to find help. On the third day, dejected, he decided to give up. Then all of a sudden he heard his name being called. He looked up and saw a missionary who had been in his village ten years before. Overjoyed, Prem told her his predicament. She was able to take him to the YWAM base, where he relayed the news about the team.

It just so happened that the next day a group from YWAM was having lunch with the American ambassador. They told him about Lis and the team, and he immediately called his consular for help. Later the consular admitted that the only reason he intervened so fast was because he had gotten the call from the ambassador. If he had been contacted by the YWAM missionaries, he would have left it for a week or so, in which time the team may have given in and signed the papers.

The following day the consular, along with a YWAM leader and an influential Nepali Christian man, drove to find the team. Just before they arrived, Lis had desperately cried out to God for help. She and the team were threatened with a beating unless they confessed to the crimes. It seemed there was no way out. Only a few minutes after Lis prayed for God to save them, the car drove up with the consular and the others. She looked up to heaven and said a silent prayer of thanks.

The local judge and lawyers were intimidated by this high-level group from Kathmandu and could not understand how they knew about the team in prison. The consular convinced the local authority to have a proper trial, and they were able to find the team a top lawyer who made the six-hour journey from the city.

After nine days in prison, the team was released on bail. This meant that they could still be sentenced and had to return to the village every month to sign in. They were not off the hook completely, but Lis was free to travel in and out of the country.

That was when I reached Lis in Kathmandu by phone. She said she would let me know when a new trial date was set. But it kept on being delayed and reset for months. Every time I heard a new date, concern crept up on me. Would Lis be imprisoned this time? The fear was like a stone in the pit of my stomach.

One evening I'd had enough. I wanted peace. I needed to be able to trust Elisabeth into God's hands. So I went to my room and sat on my bed. Full of emotion, I spoke to my heavenly Father.

"Lord, if it is your will, I release Elisabeth to go to prison," I prayed through my tears. I came to the point of realizing that if Lis did go to prison but was in God's will, she was in the best place. He would work all things together for good. As I prayed that prayer, which seemed so hard at the time, I felt a sense of release. God gave me peace. Lis was in God's hands, and whatever happened, I could trust him. This was the step I needed to take to release my daughter's future to the Lord. Then the peace came.

Thankfully, my fears of Lis going back to prison were never realized, in part because of the international effort to help the team. Lis was American and Swiss, and another girl was English and Dutch. The influential Nepali man contacted senators in the United States and members of Parliament (MPs) in the UK to put pressure on the Nepali government to change the law about evangelism. A delegation of two MPs and representatives from the US Senate went to Nepal. A year and a half after their imprisonment, the law was changed and Lis and the team were released from their charges, and hundreds of other Christians were freed from prison.

ELISABETH IN NEPAL

I learned many lessons through Elisabeth's experience in prison. I started to know deep down that Romans 8:28 is really true, that "God causes all things to work together for good to those who love God, to those who are called according to His purpose" (NASB).

• • •

Lis had helped start YWAM Nepal, where there are now over three hundred staff members. They have planted approximately 250 churches. One Nepali man who trained in the first Discipleship Training School (DTS) has been on national TV and is a positive voice in the nation. Many men and women of influence and authority in the nation were trained in YWAM schools in Nepal, and others have gone to different countries to share the Good News.

I had felt God tell me he would give me the nations as an inheritance, as it says in Psalm 2. As I relinquished Lis to work in Nepal, God gave me a great love and desire to pray for that country and people. It was a privilege to be part of what God was doing in the world while seeing his destiny for Lis being fulfilled. He was able to look after her better than I ever could. Little did I know that this was just the beginning. I would have to hold onto this lesson again and again as my children pursued the call of God on their lives in dangerous and faraway places. But first, how did this story begin?

Principles to Live By

- Prayer is the first thing we can do as we trust the Lord with our children.

- Giving our children back to the Lord is a continual process.

- We can pray honestly through our tears, fears, and other emotions.

- God will give us a heart for the nations as we pray for our children and their call.

2

FROM SWEDEN AND SWITZERLAND

You hem me in—behind and before;
you have laid your hand upon me.
—Psalm 139:5

It was a cold winter's evening in Sweden in the 1940s, and I was at home waiting for my dad and two older brothers to return from a church meeting. Mother was stitching by the fire, and I quietly played until I heard the sound of voices and steps coming up our stairs. They burst into the room excitedly.

"What happened?" I asked, running up to my brothers.

"We gave our lives to Jesus," said Kenneth, age twelve.

He went on to tell me what the preacher said and what had happened to him and my other brother, Olle, ten years old. Their eyes were bright, and as they talked, they seemed to have a new joy and peace about them. I knew I wanted what they had. Mother saw me captivated at what my brothers were saying and asked if I, too, wanted to invite Jesus into my heart.

"Yes!" I replied without a doubt.

With a big smile, she put down her stitching. "Let's do it now. Come, and we'll pray."

Taking my hand, she took me into her bedroom where we knelt at the side of the bed.

"Lord Jesus, please be Lord of my life and forgive me of my sins," I solemnly prayed, repeating the words after Mother with my hands clasped together and eyes tightly shut. In simple faith I received Jesus as Savior.

After that time, my faith grew and I knew Jesus loved me. My best friend and classmate Rose-Marie was also a Christian. We went to church together and were baptized at the same time, sang in the string band (a group of singers accompanied by mainly stringed instruments), and helped out at services in other villages. I loved music, and Rose-Marie asked if she and I could play our guitars and sing Christian songs at school. Permission was granted, and Rose-Marie and I performed for our class, hoping that everyone would be touched by the songs about Jesus and seeds would be sown. Instead, some classmates mocked and laughed at us and our faith. Thankfully I had Rose-Marie by my side, and we could encourage each other, so I was not alone in the humiliation. But this was a test for me: would I give up my reputation for the name of Jesus? I learned in a small way what, years later, my children could face as they proclaimed the name of Jesus in other countries.

Church was a major part of my family's life. My parents, Martin and Aina Randén, grew up in Smålandsstenar,

Sweden, and were active in the Mission Covenant Church, later embracing the Pentecostal revival that came to the area. I know I have reaped an inheritance from my forefathers' obedience to God. As it says in Deuteronomy 5, God blesses the children of those who love him and follow his commandments. My great-great-grandfather was influenced by a revival in his area in the 1800s, and in the early 1900s my grandfather was a leader in a mission organization that became part of the Swedish Mission Covenant Church.

GUNILA'S PARENTS, AINA & MARTIN RANDÉN

My dad, with his beautiful tenor voice, was active as a soloist, choir director, and string band leader. He also had a heart to share Jesus. He was an outgoing entrepreneur and owned a parquet flooring factory. He loved and cared for his family while also being involved in local government. My mother was a great cook and very hospitable, welcoming many guests into our home while faithfully caring for her family.

Our happy family life was about to get more exciting as Dad announced that we were going to immigrate to America. I was fourteen when we left the shores of Sweden. It was on this journey that I learned another lesson in trusting my heavenly Father.

GUNILA LEAVING FOR USA, 1953

It was a gray rainy day in October 1953 when we boarded the *Braheholm* headed for Boston. We were the only passengers on the ship. The voyage took eleven days, one more day than was expected because we hit a huge storm, the worst the *Braheholm* had been in. I remember looking out into the ocean and seeing waves as big as mountains rising and falling, our ship quaking under the power of the sea.

Despite the seriousness of the storm, I didn't feel afraid. I was reminded that we were in the hands of the Creator. He was in control of the storm and our lives. The captain was amazed that our family did not miss meals, even on the worst day of the storm. I was in awe of the power and size of the ocean, and in awe of the God who created it all. To have peace in the middle of a storm was practice for years ahead. I would count on these lessons of peace and trust when I let my children go and they would face the storms of life.

In Boston our ship was searched for smuggled goods because Sweden was near Russia and the Cold War was going on. No contraband was found, and we were able to disembark. My dad bought a car, and we spent a month sightseeing and traveling across the country to the state that was to be our home, California. On the way, we saw the mighty Niagara Falls and the beautiful Carlsbad Caverns. We also learned more English. Once we wanted ice cream and we saw a metal container that said "ice." My brother, thinking it must contain ice cream, put in a coin, and out came a big ice block. We laughed, realizing we had lots to learn!

This new land was bountiful and beautiful, but when we eventually arrived in Pasadena, California, my dad's dream of a new start was dashed. He had been sponsored by a friend in California who also had a parquet flooring business. But before we arrived, the business went bankrupt. Dad had no employment and a family of six to feed. Not one to give up easily, he worked different jobs and later bought a Swedish Bakery.

We attended Immanuel Christian Assembly in downtown Los Angeles, where the pastor was Swedish and many Swedish friends went. The church was quite similar to the one I had come from in Sweden, and I felt right at home. Little did I know that going to Immanuel Christian Assembly would play a very important role in the rest of my life. It was there that I would meet the man who would become my husband, Hans Baumann.

Hans was born near Zurich, Switzerland, in 1927. He had two older sisters, Annemarie and Ida, and one younger, Lotti. He was a man of adventure. In 1949 Hans made a trip to Sweden after learning his trade, cabinet making. At that time Europe was still recovering from the ravages of the Second World War, but Sweden seemed untouched. The country was a breath of fresh air to Hans, and he decided to go back and live there. He moved to Sweden, where he learned the language fluently.

After three and a half years, Hans was ready to move on from Sweden. With another Swiss friend, he decided to immigrate to Canada. They arrived by boat in New York and then traveled by train to Winnipeg. Hans found work as a cabinet maker and saved enough to go skiing in the Canadian ski resort of Banff before moving on to Vancouver, BC, where he spent ten months. Hans's desire to see the world wasn't satisfied, so he took a ship to Honolulu, Hawaii. He loved it there and hoped to stay, but he just couldn't find work. "They don't like you here because you're not local. Go to the mainland, and you'll get work," a friend advised.

So after three weeks he flew to Los Angeles, California. Hans didn't know a soul there, but as he walked out of the airport, he found two buses, one going to Hollywood and the other to downtown. He chose the bus going downtown and ended up staying at the YMCA. There he contacted the Carpenters Union to find work. His first job was with Illig

Construction Company, and thirty-four years later he retired from this company as one of their superintendents.

Hans was born into a Lutheran family. He had high morals and joined a Christian temperance organization in Switzerland called the Blue Cross. Although he was brought up as a Christian, he didn't have a personal relationship with God. One evening, as he was looking out of his window in downtown Los Angeles, his eyes were drawn to a huge neon sign above the Church of the Open Door. The sign said "Jesus Saves."

What does "Jesus saves" mean? he pondered.

The question was to be answered when a friend invited him to Immanuel Christian Assembly in downtown Los Angeles. There Hans heard the salvation story with fresh ears. He had known God for a long time, but he felt there had been something missing. One evening when he was all alone, he knelt on the floor in his room and gave his heart to the Lord. He was twenty-eight years old and from then on became very involved in my church.

At the same time, my life was busy with school and church. I learned English well and, still wearing my hair in long blond braids, graduated from John Muir High School at the Rose Bowl Stadium in Pasadena in 1957. With my straight A's, I wanted to study chemistry and maybe become a medical researcher. Marriage was not on my mind, but that was soon to change.

As I look back at this time in my life, I see how God was shaping me to trust him in every circumstance. He had given me loving Christian parents that guided me as I learned to know him more, read his word, and pray. He helped me to trust him while persecuted at school, going through the storm in the Atlantic Ocean, and starting afresh in America. I had chosen him, above all else, and in my decision to follow Jesus, I was finding life. Truly he had hemmed me in, behind and before. He had laid his hand upon me and was about to give me a very good gift.

Principles to Live By

- Learning to release our children into God's hands begins by putting our lives into those same hands.

- Our experiences, including those when we were young and those involving the storms of life, bring a grace that we can lean on when letting our children go.

3

A COUPLE BECOMES A FAMILY

Children are a heritage from the LORD.
—PSALM 127:3–4 NKJV

RUNNING DOWN the steps of the lavish Beverley Hills mansion, I saw Hans waiting for me in his beige Ford Mercury. It was late afternoon, and I had just finished work, looking after the daughter of the film star Peter Lorre.

Catching a glimpse of Hans by his car made my heart leap. He was so handsome—tall with dark hair and hazel eyes. I was still only seventeen, and working for Peter Lorre was my summer job before I started college in the fall. A friend from church also worked for the Lorres, and she had gotten me the job. Hans offered to pick me up sometimes, and I was grateful for the ride.

I loved spending time with him. He had become good friends with my brother Kenneth through church, as they had a common passion for skiing. The three of us loved classical music, so once in a while we would grab a bag of Danish pastries from the bakery and head off to the Hollywood Bowl to attend a concert.

Though Hans was twelve years older than me, the more time we spent together, the more I realized I really liked him. And I was hoping he felt the same.

One summer evening after church, the young people headed off to Van de Kamp's, a local bakery and restaurant. I positioned myself opposite Hans, and we played footsie under the table, chatting away normally above the table as if nothing was going on. I was letting him know that if he was interested, I was.

I soon started college, but I kept seeing a lot of Hans. In November 1957 he decided to go on a mission to Liberia to help build a leprosy rehabilitation facility. Our church supported missionaries in Liberia, and help was needed with construction. Here Hans could combine Christian service and adventure with his profession.

The night before Hans left, he came round to my family's house for a meal. Later he took me out for a drive. We drove up to the foothills of Altadena to a lookout over the city. There we talked about our hopes and dreams for the future. Hans was excited about going to Liberia, and I promised to pray for him and write often. Just before we drove home, he leaned over and gave me a kiss. My heart soared and our relationship was sealed.

The next day Hans flew to Liberia via New York. In New York he found a shop that would record him speaking onto a record. He sent it to me so I could hear his voice. I prayed for him every day, and for his mission and the people of Liberia. I eagerly awaited his letters. I didn't realize at the time that this would be a pattern of things to come—my family members would go out to the nations, and I would cover them in prayer from home and communicate by letter writing.

God truly answered my prayers and looked after Hans. One morning he had woken up in the jungle and his left leg was completely swollen. He guessed it was a spider bite, but there was no antidote at the leprosy rehabilitation facility. All he could do was get on the ham radio and contact other missionaries to ask them to pray. Within a few hours his leg miraculously healed, and he had no other side effects from a bite that could have proved fatal.

After eight months Hans returned to California. We knew we wanted to get married. The eight months apart had made our feelings for each other stronger. "You know he's much older than you," my dad said one day. It was more of an observation than a judgment. Dad just wanted to make sure I knew married life would be an adjustment. He was glad that Hans was a good worker with a steady job and could provide for me. "I know," I said with a smile.

We became engaged in March 1959 and were married a few months later, on August 1, Switzerland's national holiday, and a month before my twentieth birthday. The timing worked out well, as my parents were soon to move back to Sweden because business was better there. Olle and Bert (my younger brother) had gone back earlier to study and work. Kenneth was married by this time and would follow in a few months after finishing his studies at UCLA.

Our wedding was at Immanuel Christian Assembly. I wore a tulle and lace wedding dress with a big hoop skirt. My long blond hair had lost its braids; instead, I fashioned it in a bun on top of my head. My father sang "Ich Liebe Dich" (I love you) as an expression of the Swiss groom to his Swedish bride. Dad's strong voice soared in church where many friends had gathered on that hot evening.

WEDDING DAY, 1959

After our honeymoon I got a job at Prudential Insurance Company and enjoyed learning to cook and keep home. When I became pregnant, Hans and I decided to travel to Sweden to have the baby there. I was young and still felt attached to my parents and missed them. They had built a beautiful house by a lake near Goteborg. It had a spacious living room and a huge fireplace where petrified wood from America was mixed among the rocks from the property. The views over the lake were breathtaking. I enjoyed being back in Sweden, sitting in the sun, walking in the forest, and tasting Mom's great cooking while patiently waiting the baby's arrival.

I was overdue when my contractions started at the end of July. Hans drove me to the hospital.

"Why are you here?" the nurse asked as we waited at reception.

"Isn't it obvious?" Hans smiled, pointing to my large belly.

Elisabeth was born a few hours later, on July 29, 1961, weighing eight pounds, eleven ounces. As I held her in my arms, I thanked God for her. I couldn't believe I was a mother! Elisabeth seemed so small and fragile even though she was a healthy size for a newborn. I stayed for seven days in the hospital, learning how to nurse and look after my baby daughter.

We returned to California when Elisabeth was two months old. Hans was anxious to get back, and we moved to a triplex. Our neighbors were two young families from church. It was a happy time, three mothers with young children, enjoying our families and friendship with each other.

Elisabeth was dedicated to the Lord at our church. We wanted to follow the biblical example in Mark 10:16 of bringing our children to Jesus and having him bless them. God said in Exodus 34:19 that "the first offspring of every womb belongs to me," and this became a scripture for me to hold on to when our daughter later fully dedicated her life to serve the Lord.

When Elisabeth was about one and a half, I became pregnant again. "We are having another one," I told Hans with a smile when he came home from work.

"Wonderful!" he replied with a laugh, giving me a big hug.

Sadly, at ten weeks something went wrong. I woke up feeling ill, which I put down to morning sickness, but when I went to the bathroom I realized I was bleeding. Throughout the day I kept on bleeding. I had miscarried our baby. Later Hans and I held each other close. I was depressed, devastated that I had lost a child. I felt numb and leaned on the Lord, who healed and restored me, giving me assurance that he does what is best.

Three months later I became pregnant for a third time. Thankfully everything was okay, and Daniel was born at St. John's Hospital, Santa Monica, on December 14, 1963. At the time of his birth, there was a break in the Baldwin Hills Dam, a large dam in Los Angeles. I have wondered if it was a prophetic sign that out of Dan's life the Lord would send living water to many nations.

Our daughter Christina was born at the same place on May 20, 1968.

I loved each of my children deeply, but for some reason I longed for a fourth child. I discussed it with Hans, and he wasn't so keen. One morning, as I was praying about my desire for four children, I felt God speak to my heart: "You already have four children. One is in heaven." My eyes filled with tears as I realized that God was saying the miscarried baby was in heaven, and one day I would meet him or her. From that day on I was satisfied with having three children on this earth. I have also realized that without the miscarriage,

Dan would not be here to share his story and life, bringing people to know Jesus in many nations.

The Lord had now birthed a new generation that would be part of furthering his kingdom. As I enjoyed motherhood and as Hans loved his family while faithfully working in construction, we had no inkling of what was to come. I had not pursued a career, but being a wife, mother, and homemaker was my full-time job, and I loved it and was fulfilled. Hans and I liked to live frugally, within our means, and we were grateful that his salary supplied our needs. We could even save some and take trips to Europe to see the grandparents. We learned to be content with what we had, not "keeping up with the Joneses," and the benefit of my staying home with the children gave them a safe and secure place to grow up.

Our children are a heritage from the Lord, yes, a reward from him. Children born in one's youth are like arrows in the hands of a warrior and are blessings from the Lord (Ps. 127:4–5). We wanted him to direct each life (arrow) in his desired direction and to his desired target, that they would serve God's purpose in their generation. It was our big responsibility to pray and do all we could to raise our children to love the Lord, but parenting was not as easy as I imagined. We also needed help from the Lord as a couple, to learn to walk in unity, aligning our marriage to godly principles and nurturing it.

Principles to Live By

- Praying for our children and communicating regularly with them is an important role in their stability and support.

- Releasing our children into God's purposes starts with an initial dedication of them when they are born, seeing them as gifts from God. It is never too late for this.

- As parents, we trust that our children are a heritage from the Lord, and we do our best to be good stewards of their lives.

4

LEARNING FAMILY VALUES TOGETHER

Train a child in the way he should go, and
when he is old he will not turn from it.
—PROVERBS 22:6

HANS AND the children were ready to go. I had checked the children's bags, and now I just had to pack my own. We were about to leave for a six-week vacation to Sweden and Switzerland. The children were eager for a hike in the Swedish mountains, and we all had backpacks for the occasion.

It was 1977. Elisabeth was fifteen, Dan thirteen, and Christina nine. We were a motley crew arriving at the airport the next day with our backpacks filled with what we needed for a few weeks in Europe. We flew to Amsterdam, Holland; spent a day sightseeing there; and then boarded a ferry to Goteborg, Sweden. As the sun rose the next morning, we went out on deck to see the view. My heart leapt as I saw the archipelago off the coast of Sweden. We were close to the city of my birth, and I was excited.

After a few days we were joined by Kenneth and his family in Lofsdalen in the northern part of Sweden for our hiking holiday. The rolling hills were so different from the sharp, rugged mountains of the California Sierras where we had backpacked with the children in the past. Our children later told us that though hiking was not always their favorite vacation mode, they were grateful for the experience as it prepared them for trekking to an eye clinic in Afghanistan or to an unreached people in the Himalayas. God knew that our lifestyle was a training ground for the mission field.

READY FOR BACKPACKING IN SWEDEN, 1977

By 1964 we had moved from the triplex to a three bedroom bungalow in Manhattan Beach, a five-minute drive from the ocean. As soon as we moved in, we wanted it to be a house of hospitality. We would occasionally have visiting preachers and missionaries stay with us because we lived only fifteen minutes from Los Angeles International Airport. It was the perfect location for people traveling in and out of the country, and we heard many exciting missionary stories.

We also wanted our home to be a place of refuge and security for our children, where we could nurture and listen to them and be their number-one encouragers. Hans and I learned this through trial and error. I read books on child rearing, but in the end I found the biggest impact on me as a mother came when I drew close to God and let him change me. I loved motherhood, but I was not good at discipline. I was too lenient. I would get frustrated and not know how to deal well with whining and manipulation by the children. Hans, a strong disciplinarian, and I were not always in unity, and I had to learn to submit to Hans, which helped the peace in the family.

One day Elisabeth and Dan had been fighting. Hans was at home, and he'd had enough of their screaming. My heart melted as I saw their scared little faces as they entered the kitchen from where Hans had called them. "This behavior is not acceptable. Both of you will go to your rooms, and you won't be going to Disneyland with your friends on the weekend."

"No, Hans, that is too much," I said, disagreeing with the form of punishment. The children looked from me to their dad, imploring me with their eyes, realizing I was now their ally. Hans didn't give in and sent the children off to their room.

Later he sat me down. "*Älskling*," he said, using the Swedish word for darling, "we need to be in agreement concerning the children." I knew he was right, but at the same time part of me was fighting submission to him when I didn't always agree with his decisions.

Eventually, through the teaching I received at church and by yielding to God's work in me, my heart changed. I gave my desire for control of the children and Hans over to the Lord, trusting that God who started a good work in me would help me to change. It was a process. But slowly and surely, as I surrendered, God made it easier. As Hans and I became more united, I began to see a positive effect in the children.

Another positive influence in the lives of our children was their involvement in youth group at church. We felt it important to encourage them to be with their Christian friends, and we would always try to be available to drive them to youth group. I was aware that Hans and I were examples and models to our children. I believe our faithfulness in church and serving there had a good influence on them. If we wanted our children to follow the Lord, it was our responsibility to give them something good to imitate.

Almost every year I would take the children to our church camp at Sa-Ha-Le in Big Bear, in the mountains near Los Angeles. It was a special place for me because I had met the Lord there as a teenager, soon after I arrived from Sweden. The children loved going; they could ride horseback and swim and were surrounded by friends. The daily meetings with worship, teaching, and prayer greatly influenced their lives. Christina gave her heart to the Lord at the camp when she was six years old.

My delight was to pray, at home and with others. In one prayer group we went through the book *Operation World,* praying for all the countries of the world. It took years. This fanned my interest for the lost, and I had an atlas readily available to check where different peoples lived. I also learned to use God's Word to praise and pray. The Lord would give me guidance and encouragement through his Word for my children, highlighting a scripture applicable to the occasion and adding his peace. I would write it down and refer back to his promises in moments of doubts or questions. His Word is a sure foundation for our lives!

Reading was something both Hans and I enjoyed. I especially liked missionary biographies, and Elisabeth also found a book at home that influenced her. Called *Anointed for Burial,* it was about missionary work in Cambodia.

The years of raising children passed by quickly. My great joy was to see them grow in wisdom and stature and in favor with God and men (Luke 2:52). As the children were growing up, God was teaching me how to trust them into his hands. It was a process to let go of them and let them learn by themselves to obey and follow his voice and desire for their lives. This was really imprinted on me when we were camping one day at the beach. Hans and I were in deep conversation with friends when my attention was suddenly caught by the sound of shouting.

"Elisabeth almost drowned," Christina said as she came running to us.

I rushed down to the water to find my daughter throwing up on the beach, panting, and trying to catch her breath. She was only twelve and had been caught in a riptide that pulled her out to sea. Thankfully the lifeguard saw her and dove into the ocean to save her life. "Elisabeth, thank God you are okay," I said as I quickly wrapped a towel around her shaking body.

Later that night, when all the children were safely tucked into bed, what happened at the beach really hit me. I felt a fear rising in me for the safety of our children. I knew there were dangers in this world and that I could not protect them all the time. I was clutching onto my children, but I couldn't hold tight enough to keep them safe. All I could do was cry out to God to help me. Living in fear was not his will. Slowly, God eased my hands open, and I was able to give control over to him.

I had to let go and trust my children into God's care. Ultimately, this was the best for them because their heavenly Father could be with them at all times—and I could not. He was always watching over them and fulfilling his purpose in their lives. I am forever grateful that all our children grew up following the Lord. Hans and I had done some training with God's grace and help, but it was God's destiny for them and their personal desire to follow and be obedient to the Lord that led them to serve him in far-off places.

Principles to Live By

- Our family lifestyle is preparation for God's will for our children's future.

- Important ingredients in nurturing future world-changers include giving children opportunities to hear exciting missionary stories and being their number-one encouragers.

- Unity in the marriage relationship can provide a strong foundation for the security and future release of our children.

- Letting children go is a process. It includes realizing that we can't always hold on tight enough to keep them safe.

5

LEAVING THE NEST

*No one who puts his hand to the plough and looks
back is fit for service in the kingdom of God.*
—Luke 9:62

DRYING MY hands on a dish towel, I heard our yellow
Toyota truck pull out of the driveway with Elisabeth at the
wheel. She had recently passed her driving test and was going
to church. I smiled and waved good-bye, saying a silent prayer
for her safety on the road. This was the first time she was driving without Hans or me in the car with her, another lesson in
learning to let go.

Elisabeth didn't know what she was going to study at
college after high school. I had heard about Youth With A
Mission at a spiritual leadership conference at our church,
where one of the speakers was Loren Cunningham, founder
of YWAM. We learned about their six-month discipleship

course and wondered if Elisabeth would be interested. After talking it over, she decided to apply. I thought it would be a good opportunity for Elisabeth to take a year to find direction for her life.

Over dinner of Swedish meatballs and potatoes, we discussed Elisabeth's decision. We had heard both positives and negatives about YWAM, so we wanted to make sure Elisabeth was prepared. "Just check everything out and make sure it is according to the Bible. You can always come home if you don't feel comfortable," Hans said.

Elisabeth got a job at a local restaurant to raise funds, and by September 1979 she was ready to go to Kona, Hawaii. It was with a tear in my eye that I waved good-bye to her at LAX, knowing that I wouldn't see her for six months. She was excited for the new adventures to come, and I wished I had had such an opportunity when I was younger. It seemed so thrilling to be going somewhere to be taught the ways of God and serve the Lord with like-minded young people.

I was hoping that Elisabeth would see that missions could be fun, although at that point I had no idea it would be the path she would choose for her life. Growing up, she had been put off by missionary work after seeing two middle-aged women from our church come back from Africa on furlough every four years. They seemed old-fashioned to a free-spirited, sixteen-year-old California girl. Thankfully, in YWAM, Elisabeth soon found out that missions could be exciting and wonderful; she didn't have to become serious or boring to be part of it.

Once in Kona, Elisabeth quickly adjusted to her new life. In addition to lectures, prayer and worship times, and "flock groups" (small groups), she had to jog three miles three times a week, share a room with seven other girls, do work duties, and eat "birdseed" (granola) and yogurt for breakfast. She would write home often, and her letters were filled with all she was learning. "God is changing me from the inside out," she said in one of her letters. I could see that she was having a great time, and my mixed emotions turned to gratefulness that she was doing well. I knew the best thing for her now, in the beginning of her life, was to forge a deep relationship with Jesus. She would build on this foundation for the rest of her life.

After three months in Kona, Elisabeth moved to Honolulu for her outreach phase. Just before the end of her Discipleship Training School, we got another letter from her. "I am thinking of doing another school after my DTS. It's called a School of Evangelism (SOE)," she wrote. Whereas the DTS had been focused on personal discipleship as well as missions, the SOE was a school to prepare people for more long-term missions. Elisabeth was unsure, though, if God wanted her to go, because she didn't have enough money for the school, another six-month course. She said she was going to pray with the elders on the base for direction, and Hans and I wrote back promising to pray as well.

Eventually, Elisabeth felt she had a green light to go ahead, and together we trusted the Lord for his provision. It was at this point that God spoke to Elisabeth through Genesis 12. This is the account of the promise to Abraham that he was to leave his family and God would bless him and make him a blessing in the world. This scripture has also comforted me as one after another of my children have left and gone to serve the Lord in other countries.

Elisabeth had a couple of free weeks between her two courses, and Hans and I decided that I would visit her in Hawaii. Seeing my daughter at the airport was rewarding. She was definitely the same girl who left us six months earlier, but now she had a good tan and a deeper maturity. For the first time our roles were reversed, and she was looking after me. She showed me around Honolulu and how to get by in their cramped living conditions.

We didn't stay there for long, but took a flight over to Kona. There we went to the Kings Mansion, where she had done her training. The Kings Mansion is an old colonial house set on a mountain slope surrounded by lush vegetation, palms, plumeria trees, and fruit trees. "I like seeing where you were living, because I was praying for you there," I said to Elisabeth as we walked around the building. It has always helped knowing the surroundings the children were staying in, to better understand their lives. Later Hans and I visited them in the different countries where they were working.

Elisabeth had a dangerous experience while in Honolulu. She had been hiking up a mountain with a group of friends. They came to the top of the path, gazing in awe at the beautiful view of Honolulu and the ocean beyond. Four of them, including Elisabeth, decided to go to the top, where there was no trail. They got up without too much difficulty, but coming down proved to be a problem. The four lost their way, and suddenly they were on a steep section of the mountain jutting down to a cliff below. It was muddy and slippery. They couldn't go back, and the way ahead seemed impossible; it was hard to even get a foothold. They discussed what they should do. It was tempting to just sit where they were, but they had to move forward if they wanted to get down. But to take another step could prove fatal. With great courage, the four slowly made their way, clinging to the mountain. Sometimes Elisabeth would stretch out to what looked like a sturdy tree for support, but as she held it in her hands, it would pull away from the ground. Eventually, after much sweat and precision, they made it back, each of them thankful to be on flat, solid ground.

When I was visiting, we discussed what had happened because it had shaken her up. "But Mom, God spoke to me through it. We have to trust God for each step in our lives, and we can't hold onto false securities—like the trees that gave no support. The way may seem rough and dangerous, but intimacy with God will get us through," she said. I was touched and helped myself by her insight. Even though she had been in a dangerous situation, I knew God had used it to teach her a valuable lesson.

My two weeks were up all too soon, and Elisabeth started her SOE, without the finances to cover everything. At home we decided to have a garage sale and see how much we could raise for her outreach fund for airfare to Singapore and Indonesia.

"I'm going to sell my TV," Dan said one morning.

"That's great, Dan," I replied, touched that he was willing to sell his prized possession for his sister. Hans also helped by selling some building material he had stored, and altogether we were able to raise $300 toward Elisabeth's flight.

Hans and I were not rich but had a secure income. This was a new arena of faith for us as well, to prove God's promise in Philippians 4:19: "And my God will meet all your needs according to his glorious riches in Christ Jesus."

A couple of weeks after we sent the money, we got a joyful letter back from Elisabeth. "Thank you for the money. Guess what? My flight was reduced by $80, so I was able to help pay for another friend to get her ticket with my extra $80," she wrote.

"Freely you have received, freely give," I said to myself with a smile as I read her letter. Elisabeth was following this principle from Matthew 10:8, and God was showing that he was faithful. The rest of her fees came in miraculously—some from friends and some from people who didn't even know her need but wanted to give, prompted by the Lord.

During the SOE, God continued to speak to Elisabeth about her future. She wrote to us saying she was thinking of going back to Honolulu as a YWAM staff member and would see where things went from there. Before moving back to Honolulu, she came home for a short time to Manhattan Beach. It seemed she had just arrived when suddenly we were packing her bags again. This became very much part of our lives—welcoming our children home, and then saying good-bye again all too soon. What made it easier was that I knew our children were following the Lord, loving and serving him. Despite the financial costs and the pain of separation, we were always rewarded by the joy of knowing our children were part of bringing God's kingdom on earth.

For some mothers there is a deep fear associated with surrendering their children's future to the missionary call of God on their lives. It is somehow more attractive to bless them in a secure teaching or ministering role at home than to see them embarking on a journey to unknown territories full of unexpected hazards. These times demand a stretching experience in a mother's prayer life, and a realization that she will not be able to rush to the rescue the way she did when her children were small.

My part was now to support, pray, and communicate. Lots of letters and cards were written in the early years, and sometimes a phone call. Later we could fax and then e-mail, and using cheaper phone services helped us to keep in contact and learn of prayer needs and praise reports. Another reason for good communication was that I became the "banker," channeling support funds and letting them know what was available. It was not always easy to get money to foreign countries, but American Express helped, and now there are ATMs which make things much easier.

God was also gracious to me in confirming Elisabeth was going in the right direction. While home after the SOE, we went hiking as a family for a week in the Sierras. On the last day I was lagging behind, thinking and praying for Elisabeth and her future. I was taking my time admiring the scenery and the huge trees, the sound of birdsong, and the cool breeze on my face. Suddenly a verse came to my mind from Luke 9:62: "No one who puts his hand to the plough and looks back is fit for service in the kingdom of God."

As I thought about the verse, I felt God was saying that it was good for Elisabeth, who had started out well, to go forward in this high calling of God to "preach the good news to all creation" (Mark 16:15). I felt a peace in my heart, and I praised him for speaking. With renewed energy I caught up with the others. Later I shared with Hans what I felt God had said, and we both got excited about Elisabeth's future.

I realized that she would probably not get an education by the world's standard, but I knew she was getting great training in YWAM. She was learning to depend on God and to work with people, and she was learning leadership skills. She was also getting on-location training about new cultures and religions, experiencing a bigger world. *Education* according to *Webster's* is "the process of training and developing the knowledge, skill, mind, and character." Where better to learn this than in a Christian setting, while getting to know the character of God?

For the next step, God spoke clearly to Elisabeth about where he was sending her. One afternoon while she was staffing at the Honolulu base, she had some time off and was resting in her room. As she lay on her bed, she was asking God about the country he wanted to send her to. Suddenly a thought came to mind: *Read Esther 1:1.* Not knowing what the verse said, she grabbed her Bible from her bedside table and flipped through the pages to find the passage. Immediately, the word *India* struck her. She had no idea that India was even in the Bible.

Lord, is this you speaking? she prayed.

After a while she fell into a light sleep. An hour later she woke to the sound of a radio. Her friend next door had turned it on, and the person speaking was talking in depth about a country. The country was India.

It was time for her, like Abraham, to leave her father's household and go to the land the Lord would show her. Though India was the country where Elisabeth was to spend most of her life working overseas, she and a friend, Judy Sproats, first planned to go and start a YWAM work in Nepal, where they had visited in 1981. They had been praying for Bhutan (a country northeast of India) because they knew there were very few Christians there and no missionaries. The girls felt God ask them to be the answer to their own prayers and go to the people of Bhutan. But they were not able to get into the country. Later, when they learned about a Bhutanese community living in Nepal, Lis and Judy felt they could make a start getting to know the people there.

When they arrived in Nepal on their first two-week visit, they could not find any Bhutanese people. The trip was not wasted, though, as they realized that Nepal was a strategic place to train Nepalese people to reach the Bhutanese and Tibetans in the neighboring countries. "I would love to go back," Elisabeth wrote after that visit. Little did she know that her later work in Nepal would land her in prison.

Principles to Live By

- God's Word is important for the formation of us and our children during different seasons of life. One key passage is Genesis 12:1–3, the promise to Abram that he will be a blessing to the nations as he leaves his father's house in obedience.

- As we release our children, God will bless them with insights that also deeply encourage us.

- The very real fears that a parent feels about surrendering their child's future to the call of God should be faced honestly. This is a stretching experience in our prayer life as parents.

6

FAITH VERSUS FEAR

*Those who live in the shelter of the Most High will find
rest in the shadow of the Almighty. This I declare about
the LORD: He alone is my refuge, my place of safety.*
—PSALM 91:1–2 NLT

DAN GRADUATED from high school and informed us all he
was going to a Discipleship Training School in Heidebeek,
Holland. In September 1982 our son, a skinny eighteen-year-
old, set off for ten months away. His DTS was combined with
a School of Evangelism and would include two outreaches.

I was concerned about him traveling alone, so far away.
But I was comforted by the positive effects the teaching in
YWAM had had on Elisabeth and that she had been safe in
all her travels.

"He has been to Switzerland and Sweden before. He'll be
fine," Hans reassured me as we drove back from the airport. I
hoped he was right.

Dan had decided to go abroad after hearing Elisabeth's stories and also listening to Loren Cunningham speak of peoples who had never heard of Jesus. Dan's heart was for those people. During the lecture phase of his DTS, he prayed about where he was to go on outreach. He wrote asking us to pray with him. In the end he felt directed to the state of Goa in India. Hans and I prayed and felt at peace.

God would often speak to me through Bible verses when I prayed for Dan and the girls. This time God spoke through Psalm 25:4–15. I prayed the Word for Dan and wrote in my journal: "Father, show him your ways, teach him your paths, guide him in your truth. Lord, remember your great mercy and love for Dan, for you are good, all your ways are loving and faithful. Help Dan to keep your commands and be humble, and may the fear of God be on him. May his eyes be always on you, Lord. Thank you for your promises of prosperity and an abundant inheritance for my children."

The outreach to Goa was quite an adventure for Dan, in a different and new culture. The team prayed and worshiped and did friendship evangelism, sharing Christ with hippies and others who came to the balmy beaches in Goa. Going to the bathroom in a very basic outhouse was an experience in itself. Instead of a hole in the ground, it looked like a ramp going down the back of the hut. As Dan closed the rickety wooden door and made himself comfortable, he heard the sound of snorting and shuffling at the bottom on the ramp. He jumped up with a yelp as he saw a snout sniffing its way a little too near for comfort. He realized the produce from the outhouse was food for the local pigs. Bacon did not seem so appealing anymore.

Dan wasn't put off by the lack of comfort in his surroundings, but he did lose weight, getting down to 161 pounds, which was not much for his six-foot-two frame. God spoke to him in Goa that his experience there was preparation for hardships to come.

The second outreach was more eventful, and had me on my knees praying. Dan and a team of thirty-five traveled to Beirut. YWAM Lebanon had been waiting for the right time to bring teams in, and this seemed to be it. Lebanon had been in a war situation but was in a period of ceasefire, so the team hoped things would stay calm. They had felt God clearly lead them to Lebanon when they were given an open door into the country through an invitation from the Maronite Church. They were there to help rebuild churches destroyed by previous bombings.

Just as the team arrived, however, things started heating up, and in the spring of 1983 the ceasefire ended. My son was in a war zone.

The team was able to carry on with their work despite the dangers. Dan stayed in the city, while his friend Scott Archer and some others went to work in a clinic in the north of the country. On the way home their vehicle was captured, and they were kidnapped by a guerrilla group.

When Dan and the rest of the team found out what had happened, they earnestly began to pray. The political situation in the country was volatile, and the kidnapping was serious. There was no way of knowing how long the kidnappers would keep their hostages, or if they would kill them. The team petitioned God to save their friends. God answered their prayers, and Scott and the others were released after twenty-four hours. The experience brought a reality check to Dan and also to Hans and me as his parents. This was not just a fun adventure; the battle was very real.

A few days later, on April 18, 1983, the American embassy in Beirut was bombed. I read about it in the newspaper over breakfast one morning. My heart started beating faster as I read the words *bomb* and *Beirut*. I quickly scanned the article to see if there was any news of foreigners being killed or injured. All I could do was pray that Dan hadn't been near. I knelt in my room praying, taking my worried thoughts and putting them at the foot of the cross, asking for protection for my son.

We weren't able to telephone Dan, but I hoped Dan or someone from the team would contact us if they had been involved or hurt. As the days went by, I continued to scan the news for more information. I decided to let the information fuel my prayers, not my fear, as I interceded for my son and for the peace of the country he was in. It was so important at this time to rely on the Word of God and not allow the media to bring in fear. I knew the newspapers and TV make stories more dramatic than they often are. The Word says, "He will have no fear of bad news; his heart is steadfast, trusting in the LORD" (Ps. 112:7). It was a choice not to let the media influence my emotions but to trust our heavenly Father for his peace, wisdom, and protection.

I later learned that when the bomb went off, Dan and a few others had been sitting in the meeting room of the Maronite manse (house of the minister) where they were staying. There was a loud bang and the doors flew open as the bomb exploded. "What was that?" Dan asked as the others moved toward the window to see if they could see anything. In hindsight, that was the worst thing they could have done, but at the time the team didn't know what was going on. They found out that a stolen van carrying two thousand pounds of explosives had slammed into the American embassy. Sixty-three people had been killed in the blast.

The next day Dan and a friend went to check out the situation. The embassy was only half a mile away. To get there they had to pass seven checkpoints, each manned by American soldiers who let them through. By the time they got to the building, which had been several stories, they were in for a shock. Bodies were still being carried out of the debris. Solemnly, the two boys returned to their friends and prayed for God's presence to come in the midst of this crisis.

At night the team would hear shelling. If it came too close they went down to the basement for safety. Dan seemed to take it all in stride. In a letter home he even joked that the noise reminded him of the Fourth of July in America.

Another girl from our area, Debbie Austin, was on the same outreach as Dan. When I heard the news of how bad the situation was, I would phone her mother, Jean. Together we would pray for our children, that they would be kept safe in the midst of such danger. It was comforting to pray together.

Trying not to worry was hard, but it was a choice I had to make again and again. Hans and I trusted that God had directed Dan to go to Beirut; therefore, we had to trust him to watch over our son. Dan told us that many of the other students were receiving letters from their parents telling them to come home immediately or to go somewhere safer. We knew we couldn't do this if Beirut was where God wanted Dan to be. We wrote to Dan, affirming the truth that we knew God would guide and direct him. I prayed Psalm 32:8 over Dan: "I will instruct you and teach you in the way you should go; I will counsel you and watch over you." Dan was learning to hear God's voice and be obedient to the next thing God would tell him. God's promises were both for him and for us to believe and trust in. Knowing God's promises and keeping our minds on the Lord helped keep us in perfect peace.

One day Dan and Jeff, another American, were walking in the city. The area was eerie, like a ghost town. Bottles of beer half drunk were on café tables, and food not finished on plates. It was a picture of a society who had just up and left in seconds. Dan and Jeff found themselves in front of the former Palestine Liberation Organization (PLO) headquarters, what was once a Holiday Inn. Now it looked like Swiss cheese, it had so many bullet holes in it. The boys were speechless as they slowly entered the building, where there was not a soul around. Standing in the gutted lobby, they stopped in front of the main stairwell. The building was pitch black apart from shafts of light shining through bullet holes in the walls and crashed-out windows. The pair made it up to the top of the building, the thirty-fifth floor, and stood looking over the city. They spent time taking in the view and praying for peace in the country. "It was magnificent," Dan said later, when he described the experience.

Despite the very real dangers, Dan and his friends had a fruitful time in Lebanon. Most of the expats had left the city because of the war. When the Lebanese asked them why they hadn't gone home after the bombing, their reply was, "We were asked to come for three months, and we will stay for three months." They were able to make friends with the Lebanese people very easily. These friendships led to conversations about faith. Eventually, the group decided to invite their new acquaintances to a meeting at the manse. It would be once a week, and they would explain more about who Jesus is.

The first week, seven people came. By the end of their time in Beirut, Dan and the group were welcoming over a hundred people, all eager to hear what they had to say. From those weekly meetings a church was formed, led by a new convert, and many believers kept meeting together after the team left. The ministry experience impacted Dan.

What further influenced Dan and his thoughts for the future was hearing his friend Carl Medearis, a twenty-year-old American team member, talk about his visit to Yemen. Carl had left the Lebanon outreach to join a man building latrines in Yemen. When he returned for the team debriefing, his words struck a chord in Dan. He spoke of falling in love with the Muslim people, of eating with them and living day-to-day life with them. His heart was broken for them, and he knew he was going to work with them for the rest of his life.

When Dan heard Carl speak, something clicked in him. "I want to give my heart to a people that don't know Jesus. I want to live with them and die with them, to give them my life," he later told Hans and me. Tears came to my eyes when I heard this. I was so proud of Dan, but at the same time I knew it would mean he could be going even farther away from home, to dangerous and unknown places. We had to truly let our son go, because it looked like America wasn't going to be his home for much longer.

First, however, Dan was coming back to the United States to go to college. Two months into his DTS, he felt God was directing him to return home and study for a degree after his SOE outreach. It helped that God had spoken clearly, because many of the leaders asked Dan to become a staff member on the base after he finished his outreach. It was tempting to stay, but Dan knew God had something different for him.

During this time, I was praying that Dan would know the right way and walk in it. He stuck firm to what he felt God had said and moved back home to attend El Camino Junior College, studying business. It was a joy to have him at home, and I was so impressed at the maturity he had gained from being away.

Three weeks into Dan's time at home, God spoke to Dan in a supernatural way. He was sitting in his room at home, when suddenly a name came into his mind.

Ashkabad.

Where did that come from? he wondered. He'd never heard of it before, to his recollection.

Turning to a map of the world, he tried to place the name to a country. Then he found it. Ashkabad was the capital of Turkmenistan. He knew it would be impossible to go there because it was a closed country, part of the Soviet Union. *God, is this from you?* he prayed. He stored what had happened in his heart, waiting for a time when God would make his purpose clearer. Not a word was said to Hans and me about Ashkabad at the time. We found out years later.

Dan had been praying about applying to Wheaton College in Illinois to finish his schooling. My mother was the one to encourage him. She knew that men of God like Billy Graham and Jim Elliot had been through Wheaton's doors, and she felt it would be a good training ground for her grandson. Dan was accepted and moved a four-hour flight away to the Chicago area. While he was there, God was working in my heart to trust my son more fully into God's hands.

One morning I was busying myself in the kitchen, when the phone rang. "Is this Mrs. Baumann?" asked the voice at the end of the line.

"Yes," I replied.

"I am calling from Wheaton College. Your son Daniel is in the hospital. He was involved in a football accident."

My immediate thought was to fly to be with him. I couldn't bear Dan being alone and in pain in a hospital. After I got off the phone with the college, I called Hans at work. "I need to go and be with Dan," I told him.

Hans made me calm down and think about the situation rationally. "Go and pray and see what God says," he told me.

I did what he said, and God met with me in a powerful way. "Dan is my son as well," he said. "I will be with him." Peace flooded into my heart. I realized Dan would be okay even if I wasn't there to look after him, because his heavenly Father was taking care of the situation.

It turned out Dan had broken his left arm badly. He needed three pins and two screws to put it together again. The operation took five hours. But God used the situation to speak to our son. Dan had been having a hard time at

Wheaton, and the broken arm was the final straw. As he convalesced alone, without his mother fussing over him, God started to speak.

"Does this broken arm take away my relationship with you?" the Lord asked.

Dan began to learn not to look at circumstances to judge his relationship with the Lord. Even if things were not going well, God had not disappeared or abandoned him. God used the broken arm to show my son that his relationship with the Lord was to be of the utmost importance. God also used the situation to bless Dan with deep and lasting friendships. Dan had been finding it hard to settle into college and make friendships; he was often lonely. After the accident, however, people rallied around him, and friendships grew out of that. It changed his college life for the better.

In his junior year Dan applied to join a summer outreach program. He was selected with fifteen others to go to Turkey. The fact that he was chosen to go to Turkey was an answer to another prayer. Dan knew that the Turkmen world had a rich history and stretched from Istanbul to northwest China. It included 150 million people and eight countries, one being Turkmenistan. Dan had prayed that God would direct his application for the summer outreach to go somewhere in that area. The project sent students all around the world, from Australia to Europe to Africa, and they had little choice or influence in where they went. So when Dan found out he was going to Istanbul, he was deeply touched. He felt God was confirming his call to the Turkmen people group.

While in Turkey, Dan studied the language and made friends. He felt alive in the culture, and his letters home were full of excitement at what he was seeing and learning. I could only be happy that my son was pursuing God's call on his life, as I knew there could be no greater satisfaction than following the way that God had set out before the beginning of time.

Dan graduated from Wheaton in 1987 with a degree in business administration and economics. For seven months he was back home again, working as a painter and waiting for the next step.

I prayed for him often during that time, and God encouraged me through the hymn "I'll Go Where You Want Me to Go."

> There's surely somewhere a lowly place,
>   In earth's harvest fields so wide,
> Where I may labor through life's short day,
>   For Jesus the Crucified;
> So trusting my all unto Thy care,
>   I know Thou lovest me!
> I'll do Thy will with a heart sincere,
>   I'll be what you want me to be.
>
> I'll go where you want me to go, dear Lord,
>   O'er mountain, or plain, or sea;
> I'll say what you want me to say, dear Lord,
>   I'll be what you want me to be.

I knew God would open up a place for Dan to labor in the harvest field.

During this time, Dan began to feel that God was going to send him somewhere else before going to Turkmenistan, but he didn't know where. At that time Elisabeth was home for a few weeks. One day she was on the phone with a friend. He told her about an NGO called International Assistance Mission (IAM) in Kabul, Afghanistan. He said they were accepting applications for administrators and asked if she knew anyone who might be interested.

When Elisabeth told Dan, he wondered if this was the place he should go to before Turkmenistan. It was in the same part of the world, and Dan was eligible to apply for the job because of his university degree.

God knows our future so well. He asks us to do things, and at the time it may not be clear why we have to do them. Later, if we are obedient, we often see the purpose. Dan was obedient in going to college, and the degree opened the way for a job in the area of the world he wanted to live and serve.

He applied for a position and waited for a response, working temporary jobs in California until the time came for him to leave. Weeks turned into months, but there was still no word from Kabul.

In 1988 Christina was staffing a DTS in Honolulu. She called home one day and spoke to Dan. "You need to go to India," she told him.

Christina explained she knew of a team who were living among Afghan refugees in Old Delhi. The aim was to befriend and reach the Muslims in that area. When she heard about the team, she knew Dan would love what they were doing. She was right. Dan was excited by the opportunity. But he didn't have the finances to go and assumed it wouldn't be possible, so he told Christina he couldn't go.

The next day as he was praying, he felt the Lord tell him to listen to Christina and what she was saying. He obeyed. Two weeks later, with all the money he had, he purchased a one-way ticket to India. He had no committed support but in faith made his way there. Had not the Lord faithfully provided for Elisabeth through friends, family, and the church while she was serving in Asia? So now we trusted him to do the same for Dan. It wasn't long after Dan left that our church committed to help him with some support.

Dan joined Steve Cochrane, an American from Washington State who was the YWAM leader of a team in Delhi. They lived together in a small room in the middle of a strong Muslim area and made friends with their neighbors, immersing themselves in the culture. It was a spiritually oppressive place. Dan and the others encouraged themselves in the mornings through worship and prayer, shaking off feelings of heaviness and oppression. The living/sleeping room was small and narrow, with four mattresses on the floor. They lived very simply. Dan lost fifty-five pounds in the process, through sickness and the stifling heat. The pollution was affecting his asthma, and not eating well made him weak.

Later, Hans and I saw the room he had lived in. It was off a busy street with rickshaws speeding up and down between masses of people. The temperature was almost unbearable, and the spiritual oppression in the area seemed to intensify the heat. We realized what good preparation this had been for Dan before going to Kabul, Afghanistan, because he also had opportunity to get to know Afghans, love them with Christ's love, and learn about their culture.

Dan eventually got the position as an administrator of IAM's eye hospital, NOOR, and moved to Kabul. There he found out that Delhi was the city he would be sent to by IAM to temporarily get out of the stressful atmosphere of the war zone. Dan went back to Delhi twice a year for six years. He was able to meet with old friends and feel at home in a city that he now knew well.

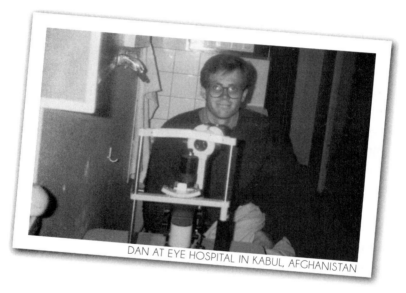

DAN AT EYE HOSPITAL IN KABUL, AFGHANISTAN

God provided and took care of all his needs, step by step. The Lord was making a way for Dan. He was also showing me that even in hardship and difficult situations, he is still there in all his fullness and with all his provision. This was wonderful to hold on to as Dan entered more turbulent and dangerous situations in Afghanistan.

As I watched my children go on short-term mission trips, and later work as full-time missionaries, I learned again and again that God is faithful and provides for all our needs. Our faith was stretched as much as our children's, as we waited for the provision to come, often wondering how God would do it.

Principles to Live By

- Praying the Scriptures for our children and recording our prayers in a journal can help us find grace to release them as well as provide a way of remembering what God has done.

- When our children are in risky situations, we must choose to trust and pray instead of worry.

- God is ultimately responsible not only for directing our children's lives but also for providing resources for that direction.

7

LEARNING ABOUT FINANCES

Give, and it will be given to you. A good measure,
pressed down, shaken together and running
over, will be poured into your lap. For with the
measure you use, it will be measured to you.
—LUKE 6:38

"THE YOUTH are going to the island of Saipan. Can I go too?" Christina asked after church one Sunday.

It was 1982, and she was only fourteen. Our church was planning a youth trip to this island in the Northern Marianas in the western Pacific. Hans and I looked at each other, knowing we didn't have enough money to send her. Dan, who was eighteen at the time and had not yet gone on his DTS, also wanted to go.

"We'd like to let you go. Let's see what God does," Hans replied, with confidence in God's ability to provide.

Hans and I prayed together about Dan and Christina going. We didn't want to let finances stop them, but we only had three hundred dollars. They needed eight hundred dollars each.

The following Sunday we talked to our children's youth pastor, Mike Jackson. "We would love for them to go to Saipan, but we can't afford to send them," I explained.

"Don't worry. Put their names on the list, and God will provide somehow," Mike said with a smile.

His faith was rewarded as the money came in from members of the church who gave to support the youth. Christina loved her first taste of serving God in another country. The team helped at the YWAM base on the island. They went on outreaches to the villages, going door to door and telling the people about Jesus. They also helped by cleaning out YWAM's chicken coups and doing other types of manual labor.

The next year Christina asked to do a Summer of Service with YWAM in Hong Kong. I knew I would have to hear from God if he wanted her to go, because again we didn't have enough money to support her trip. Plus I still felt she was very young to be traveling alone so far away and for so long. The Lord had encouraged me from 1 Samuel 16, the account of David being chosen as king of Israel. He was the youngest, and he was the one whom God wanted. While praying for Christina, I gave her back to the Lord and asked for a sign to know that it was okay for her to go to Hong Kong.

Father, I ask for a financial sign for Christina so that I will know she is supposed to go to Hong Kong and that you will provide for her and protect her, I prayed.

Later that day when Hans came home from work, he said, "I was able to sell some scrap metal today, and I made forty dollars. I think we are supposed to give it to Christina for Hong Kong."

"That's great," I replied, smiling inwardly at the Lord's answer to my prayer. The quick answer gave me peace to let Christina go.

Hans and I felt at this time that we were also to give our vacation money to Christina for the trip. When we have been obedient to give what God tells us to give for our children's mission trips, he has supplied the rest and we have not lacked.

We were learning the financial principles from the Bible:

> "Do not store up for yourselves treasures on earth, where moth and rust destroy, and where thieves break in and steal. But store up for yourselves treasures in heaven, where moth and rust do not destroy, and where thieves do not break in and steal. For where your treasure is, there your heart will be also." (Matt. 6:19–21)

> And my God will supply all your needs according to His riches in glory in Christ Jesus. (Phil. 4:19 NASB)

God loves a hilarious and generous giver. From the beginning of our marriage, we tithed and gave offerings to our Lord, which has a biblical promise of blessing. Our family experienced the fruit of this promise, seeing God's provision of our house, of money to help others in need, of tuition for college and YWAM schools, and more. As we were obedient, we found great joy in giving. It came down to a matter of the heart. We gave first and prayed for people's hearts to be touched, and then asked God to show us whom we should share our children's needs with. He was so faithful to respond, sometimes through established relationships and sometimes through people we did not know.

At the same time, I had been listening to teaching at church that solidified what I was learning. Loren Cunningham spoke on relinquishing your rights, even your rights to your children and what they do with their lives. Later, back at home, I quietly prayed through what I had heard. "Lord, I know you do all things well. I give you the rights to my children. They are yours before they are mine."

Christina, only fifteen, ended up going to Hong Kong, but not alone. My friend Peg Beven's niece Vicky was also going. She was older and promised to look out for Christina.

The eight-week trip had a big impact on Christina's life. She went to help the boat people in an area called Aberdeen and told them about Jesus. She also went with three other young women on a train ride from Hong Kong to China, smuggling Bibles into the country. The trip was very short. Vicky led the group of all teenagers, each with twenty pounds of Bibles in their bags. Thankfully no one was held up in customs. They traveled to a city, went to a restaurant, and exchanged bags with believers in a prearranged meeting. Then they got straight on the train and headed back to Hong Kong.

After high school Christina was interested in working as a flight attendant but asked God to show her if he had other plans. She felt directed to join the YWAM base in Honolulu for a DTS. Fiji was the destination for their outreach. There she lived with a Muslim family, and this was the beginning of her love for and desire to reach Muslims with the Good News.

She followed her DTS with an SOE and went on an outreach to India. When Christina arrived in Delhi, she did not like the country at first. She wrote home telling us that Steve Cochrane had picked the team up at the airport. It was over one hundred degrees as they rode in a government bus. The guest house they were staying in was very basic. Sitting in the intense heat with sweat dripping off her, trying to get used to the mass of humanity in such a crowded place, Christina prayed, *Lord, if you want me to work in a place like this, you have to speak to me.* She waited to hear if God would speak as she slapped the mosquitoes trying to bite her arms and legs. He didn't say anything at that time, but she had peace knowing that he would make the way clear.

The team planned to work in a church in Leh, a city in the Ladahk region of northern India. They decided to hike two hundred kilometers, part of the distance from Srinagar to Leh. Late one afternoon they came to Zoji La, an 11,500-foot mountain pass. The landscape was dry and rocky, and the weather a pleasant seventy degrees. The view was stunning, with majestic mountains rising up into the clear blue sky.

"Hey, it looks like a shortcut over there," Christina said to her Samoan friend Marieta.

The two of them made their way off the path, to what looked like a quicker way. Christina was ahead of Marieta when suddenly she realized that the ground beneath her was moving. It was all rubble; nothing was stuck to the ground. Even boulders were sliding down the mountain.

"Help!" she screamed as she slid toward the edge of a cliff.

Marieta called for the leader of their group, but there was nothing anyone could do. Christina was grabbing onto anything she could. Suddenly, she froze. Any false move and she could fall to her death two thousand feet below.

At that moment a truck came around the corner on the main road. The team flagged it down, and a Sikh man jumped out to see what the problem was. When he realized Christina needed help, he quickly pulled off his turban and uncoiled it. Some others from the truck joined him, tying their turbans together to make a rope. By this time Christina's arms were beginning to shake with tension from trying to keep still. In the nick of time, the turban rope came dangling down to her. With the rest of her strength, she grabbed on and was pulled up to safety.

After Christina's harrowing experience, the team gave up the idea of trekking and instead hitchhiked to their destination.

When they had settled in for the night, the team had a prayer meeting. Christina felt God speak to her. "I saved you today, but there are people here who will go to hell if they die. Are you willing to go to them? Are you willing to be the rope to pull them up?" Silently, with tears running down her cheeks, Christina committed her life to help these people, to tell them the Good News. It was the personal call she was asking for.

In her time on outreach, Christina grew to love the people of Kashmir deeply, so much so that she found it hard to leave them and come home. When Christina told Hans and I the hiking story, I gasped at the thought of my precious daughter so close to death. But again I saw God's faithfulness in protecting her and in using the situation to speak clearly to her about her future. I thanked him for his protection.

As Christina felt her heart grow for the Muslims in Kashmir, she wanted to get more training so that she could be used to her full potential to help the people. At that time, no YWAM work had been established in Kashmir, so Christina would have to pioneer it with whatever team God put around her. First she wanted to learn the Word of God better and applied for a nine-month School of Biblical Studies (SBS) in Hong Kong. There her destiny became more focused as she fell in love with Greg Watt from Canada, who was also attending the school.

• • •

Christina was our last child to go into missions. Now all our children were trusting God for their finances. As we trusted God with our finances, he supplied all our needs and our children's needs.

One way he did this was through a retirement gift. In the fall of 1989 Hans retired after thirty-four years at Illig Construction Company. By the end of his time there, Hans had served as a superintendent on various jobs. He led the building of a Georgio Armani store in Beverley Hills and the remodeling of the J. Paul Getty Museum and other special buildings. I was so proud when I heard him being praised for his hard and diligent work for the company. As a retirement gift, Hans was awarded $10,000.

"We know you are a Christian, so if you want to give it to your church, we won't deduct taxes," Hans's boss said, smiling.

We decided to do that very thing. God had blessed us so much over the years that we chose to give this blessing back. Our church was now helping to support all our children, and we could have $2,000 assigned to each of them out of the gift. God confirmed that this was the action we should take through 1 Timothy 6:18–19, in which the believers are commanded "to do good, to be rich in good deeds, and to be generous and willing to share. In this way they will lay up treasure for themselves as a firm foundation for the coming age, so that they may take hold of the life that is truly life."

We felt so proud to see Christina step out in faith. Each one of our children was taking hold of life. In different ways they were all storing up treasures in heaven.

Principles to Live By

- Giving up the rights to our children *internally* is an important step before we are called to surrender them to God's call *externally*.

- Storing treasures in heaven becomes a family affair as we join our children in giving everything to the Lord and his kingdom work.

8

FOLLOWING
GOD'S WAYS

And everyone who has left houses or brothers
or sisters or father or mother or children or
fields for my sake will receive a hundred times
as much and will inherit eternal life.
—MATTHEW 19:29

WHEN ELISABETH was single in Kathmandu, Nepal, working in often difficult circumstances, I would pray from time to time for a husband for her. My hope for my children was first that the Lord would capture their hearts and show them that he was sufficient for all their needs. I also prayed that in his time he would bring the right mate across their paths.

In 1981, when Lis was about to move to Nepal, she felt the Lord speak from Isaiah 54: "Your Maker is your husband—the Lord Almighty is his name" (v. 5). She had peace as she heard that word, and was able to lean on the Lord.

In 1984 a DTS outreach team worked in a village called Pithoragarh in the Himalayas. About thirty new converts had come to know Jesus, and a church of new believers was started. The outreach team eventually had to leave, but they didn't want to leave the church without any support and guidance. So Lis, who was the leader of YWAM in Nepal, offered to go to Pithoragarh for a two-week interim before another team arrived to take over responsibilities.

The two weeks fell over Christmas, and Lis would be staying in a schoolhouse where rats were the only other guests and there was no running water or electricity. *It's only two weeks, I can do it,* Elisabeth thought to herself. She had a kerosene stove, and the schoolmaster and his family lived on the same compound, so she wouldn't be completely alone.

When she arrived in Pithoragarh and surveyed her home, she prayed, *Okay, Lord, you said you would be my husband. Please look after me.* She then headed out to visit the villagers. Although she didn't have much money, she decided to use what she had to buy some biscuits and chai to have a little party with the church on Christmas Day.

On the way back from the market, she realized her wallet was missing. Putting down her bag, she searched through all her pockets twice, hoping against hope that she would find it. The wallet contained not only all her money but also her bus ticket back to Kathmandu. After searching everywhere, she knew her wallet was gone. She had no way to retrieve her money or her ticket and no way to make a call. She was completely stuck.

She sat down in the market and unexpectedly felt a wave of peace, banishing all anxious thoughts.

Lord, I have nothing, but I have you, and that is enough, she prayed.

She felt God speak to her. "Go to the school and carry on your ministry. I am with you."

Lis obeyed. She had come to the place of surrender and couldn't do anything in her own strength. She had to rely on God, and in her desperation he was proving that he was there. He was her husband. He was making a way.

Coming back to the schoolhouse after a long day, Lis gasped as she saw her wallet placed by the entrance of the door. She ran and opened it to see what was inside. Half the money and the bus ticket had been stolen, but there was enough to buy another ticket for the twenty-four hour bus ride back to Kathmandu. Lis knew it was a miracle that all the money hadn't been taken and that the wallet had been returned. After all, how did the thief know where the owner of the wallet lived?

During the two weeks that Lis served in the village, another two people became converts and the church was encouraged. Lis left with the best Christmas present, a deep knowledge that God was there when she needed him most.

After Lis arrived back in Kathmandu, she was asked to speak in a village. A sound system was set up, and over three hundred people came to hear her speak. The area where the people had gathered was long and narrow, and the crowd had to sit almost in a line. Lis was glad for the microphone, because it would ensure they would hear her.

Just as she was about to speak, the sound system broke down. She had to shout her entire message. When she had finished, the local pastor thanked God that he had given Lis such a loud voice. As he said this, Lis began to cry. In high school Lis had been teased for her loud voice. One day she had come home very upset. "Don't feel bad. One day God will use your loud voice," I said, trying to make her feel better. Lis now remembered what I had said many years before.

It turned out that the sound of Lis's voice was useful in villages where electricity came and went. Lis preached many times without a microphone, and everyone could hear her words. When I heard these stories, I was reminded of how we are made perfectly by God. The abilities and qualities we have are exactly enough to fulfill his calling. God made Lis in his own special way for a reason. Nothing was a mistake, nothing was wasted.

The Lord who saved Elisabeth's life more than once while she was in Nepal, proved again and again that he would be her husband and protector and provider. One day Lis was going to visit a new YWAM ministry in eastern Nepal, and she caught a bus to the village where she had been in prison. Normally she would walk straight to the back of the bus where there were seats available, but this time she agreed to an invitation to sit in the front.

A half hour later, the driver lost control and the bus skidded off the road. The passengers screamed as the vehicle fell several feet and tumbled down a steep hill. Suddenly the bus came to a standstill. Lis edged her way to the nearby door and was able to get out. She stumbled up to the road and fell to the ground, thanking God for his protection. Many passengers on the bus had been injured, and several were killed. Lis realized that if she had been sitting in the back where she had intended, she would have died. She felt God speak to her heart: "I have more for you. This was not your time."

Not long after this experience, Lis felt God say something else, that he was going to provide her with an earthly husband. She was content in her work and her singleness, and she waited for the man God would bring.

Two years later Steve Cochrane asked Lis to marry him, and she said yes. Lis and Steve had known each other for years, having both worked with YWAM in Asia. While Lis had been pioneering a base in Nepal, Steve had been pioneering a YWAM work in Calcutta and Delhi, India. When he phoned Hans and I to ask our permission to marry our daughter, we happily said yes. We had met Steve a couple of times. He had even stayed in our Manhattan Beach home. We liked him a lot and thought he would be a great match for Elisabeth.

Showing his dedication, Steve asked Lis to marry him when she still had a jail sentence hanging over her head. Although it had been a few years since she was in prison, the court case had not yet been resolved, and Lis was on bail. If she were imprisoned again after getting married, Steve would have to move near the prison and bring her food each day. He said he would gladly do this, but thankfully he never had to.

Steve and Lis were married at our church, Calvary Church of the Coastlands, in Torrance, California, on July 8, 1989. Many YWAMers from different parts of the world joined the big celebration. Elisabeth looked beautiful in a taffeta gown embroidered with lace and beads. Her friend and bridesmaid Lisa had made the veiled hair piece.

The next day Steve and Lis, with their common missions interest, traveled to Manila, Philippines, for the Lausanne II mission conference. A wonderful honeymoon followed in Palm Springs, California.

STEVE & ELISABETH, 1989

Lis and Steve sensed God directing them to a new place. They decided on Pune, India, where they would pioneer several new works. Steve led Frontier Missions and Muslim ministry for YWAM in South Asia, and eventually established over seventy church-planting teams. Lis focused on local ministry, sending teams to work in the slums around the city and in orphanages while overseeing the YWAM schools and teaching. Working together as a team, Lis and Steve supported and encouraged each other.

A young orphan woman named Suman Joshi joined the first DTS in Pune. She loved the Lord and was eager to learn. During the outreach, her team worked with the poor in a slum in Pune. Suman loved working there and later decided to enroll in a primary health care school with YWAM to help her in the work she had started. When she finished the school, she asked to speak to Lis.

NEWLYWEDS LEAVING FOR MANILA

"I know I don't have many qualifications, but can I continue to work in the slum?" she asked.

Lis was touched by her humble heart and willingly agreed, offering to help in any way. Two decades later Suman is still there. God provided a husband for her, and with his help she has transformed the slum of ten thousand people. It became known as the nicest slum in Pune, with its own school and health clinic. Although her husband has now passed away, Suman and her teams have taught over one thousand women to read using the Bible. They have delivered babies, taught basic health care, and schooled over one thousand children.

Steve and Elisabeth were following God's leading in their lives. They had foregone living near family and accumulating material possessions in the United States and were instead storing up heavenly possessions, which rust and moth do not destroy. They were living rich, fulfilling lives, seeing wonderful results in their labor. And they were impacting nations. If this was at the cost of a mortgage-free house and two cars in their garage—the American dream—in my eyes it was more than worth it.

Principles to Live By

- Trusting God with our children's lives includes trusting that he will bring the right mate to them or bring his grace in a calling of singleness.

- As we watch our children grow and be obedient to God, we can learn much through them about the fleeting value of material goods.

9

THE PILLAR OF CLOUD IS MOVING

In your unfailing love you will lead the people
you have redeemed. In your strength you
will guide them to your holy dwelling.
—Exodus 15:13

"It is our turn for an adventure," I said, smiling at Hans as I packed what we would need for four months away from home. We had so much freedom now that Hans was retired. It was March 1990, and we had carefully planned a trip abroad. It would be the first time we would see all our children in Asia serving the Lord. We felt like we knew many of their friends and coworkers through faithful communication, and now we would get to meet them face to face.

Hans and I would first fly to Switzerland for three weeks to visit his family, and then to India to meet Steve and Elisabeth. We would spend ten weeks in Afghanistan working and living with Dan and meet with Christina on our return trip through India.

When we landed at the Bombay (now Mumbai) Airport, the heat, noises, and mass of people hit my senses. I had never experienced anything like it.

"Mom, Dad, over here!" Lis shouted as we came through customs. She looked like a blond Indian in her Punjabi dress.

Lis and Steve led us to a taxi that took us to a Methodist guest house. Even though it was 1:40 a.m., there was still activity as we drove through the city. I was spellbound as I looked out the taxi window. Some people were sleeping on the sidewalks. Others lived in large communities of shacks that seemed to go on for miles.

We arrived at the guest house, and the guard opened the gate. When the receptionist was awakened, there seemed to be a problem.

"I'm sorry, we can't find the key to your room," he said.

After much discussion, we were taken to our room where the guard smashed a hole through the door to open it from the inside. Hans and I smiled to each other but didn't say a word as we entered our room.

The next day we loved all the new sites and experiences. It helped that we were looked after by our children. They showed us how to get around and made all our arrangements. It filled my heart with joy to see them happy and fulfilled in a country so different and far away from home.

After four days in Bombay we traveled three and a half hours by train to Pune, where Lis and Steve were working. We stayed with them in their flat, and they showed us the work they were leading among the Indians. We ate (and learned to like) the spicy food that the maid cooked, we lit the mosquito repellent coils before we went to bed, and we slept on beds made of plywood and a foam pad.

After two weeks we flew to Delhi and then on to Afghanistan. Dan picked us up in an old maroon Volvo, the first car he had ever owned. Being in Afghanistan was a life-changing experience. We stayed in Kabul, which is situated in a valley. The Soviet occupation had ended, and the Afghan freedom fighters were now surrounding the city, firing rockets at random. In return, the government forces fired back. Although we were in a war zone, Hans and I had a supernatural peace. Being there helped us understand how our children felt living in such circumstances. I was constantly reminded of one of my favorite verses: "Thou wilt keep him in perfect peace, whose mind is stayed on thee" (Isa. 26:3 KJV). I found this to be so true.

I helped in the office of the International Assistance Mission (IAM), the Christian NGO that Dan was working with. Hans helped with maintenance at the NOOR Eye Hospital, where Dan was an administrator.

The bombs were coming a little too close for comfort. One morning as I was working in the IAM office, a huge bang shook the ground. From the window we could see dark smoke and fire billowing furiously into the air. A rocket had hit an ammunitions truck close by. Ann Penner, the wife of the leader of IAM, and her fourteen-year-old daughter Becky, had been in a car near the blast. Miraculously, they were not hurt and were able to drive to safety.

A few days after this incident, a rocket hit the Inter-Continental Hotel, where we sometimes ate Sunday lunch with Dan and friends. Later we went to see the hotel. The rocket had made a huge crater in the parking lot, and the hotel windows were blown out.

With destruction surrounding us, I had a special desire to go up to the mountain surrounding Kabul and pray for the city. We needed to get permission from the army to do this, which took some time, but eventually we received approval.

GUNILA, HANS, AND DAN, BEFORE ROCKET HIT HOTEL PARKING LOT

Early one morning Hans and I and some others from IAM set out for the mountain. We hiked for an hour and a half to the top. There was a military outpost at the summit, and we were met by several Afghan soldiers. Instead of being hostile, they seemed glad to have visitors. They brought us sweets and tea and even asked if anyone wanted to try shooting one of their guns. I was amazed at their offer, which Hans accepted. I took a photo of Hans aiming an AK-47. He was a good marksman as a boy and had won a shooting competition in Switzerland. Now he was firing a real gun in war-torn Afghanistan—for fun.

HANS WITH AFGHAN SOLDIERS

As the sun rose higher in the sky, reflecting off the glass windows of the city below, we began to pray. I proclaimed Isaiah 40 over the city. Verse 9 felt especially pertinent: "You who bring good tidings to Zion [or Afghanistan], go up on a high mountain. You who bring good tidings to Jerusalem [or Kabul], lift up your voice with a shout, lift it up, do not be afraid; say to the towns of Judah [or Afghanistan], 'Here is your God!'" As I prayed, my heart broke for the Afghan people. And I understood in a greater way our children's love for the Muslim world.

As we hiked down the mountain, I had my photo taken in a gap between the rocks of an old wall. When I looked at the picture later, the significance of it hit me. I knew that

God was asking me to stand in the gap (Ezek. 22:30) for my children and for people around the world by interceding for them. For years I had prayed at home for peoples and countries, and now I was praying on location. It was exciting and a privilege to see the gospel bearing fruit in Asia and to meet new believers in Afghanistan.

GUNILA READING ISAIAH 40 OVER KABUL, AFGHANISTAN

After ten weeks we flew back to Delhi, where we enjoyed a week with Christina. She had recently finished her School of Biblical Studies in Hong Kong. Our four-month trip had come to an end.

Our time away had been an eye-opening look into our children's lives. It was a reward for the years of encouraging them in their work and supporting them through love, prayer, communication, and finances. To see the lives they were impacting and the Lord was renewing made it all worth it.

Hans and I had talked about doing a Discipleship Training School ourselves. We didn't think long-term missions was where we were supposed to be, but we wanted to use the rest of our years to support missionaries, and our children, in whatever way we could.

In October 1990 we took a holiday to Kona, Hawaii, and stayed at the YWAM base there. We met someone who told us about the Crossroads DTS for those thirty-five and older in Einigen (Spiez), Switzerland. The school was in German and English and was starting in January.

Was this the answer to our prayers? We had wanted to do a DTS in Switzerland to be near Hans's mother, and we knew about an English- and French-speaking school in Lausanne. But this DTS in Einigen would be perfect for us. Hans spoke German, and I would be able to learn more German through the translation.

We hastily applied and waited to hear if we were accepted. God provided for the fees and our travel expenses. Hans's sister Lotti lived with their mother in Switzerland. All four siblings would eventually inherit the house, and Lotti asked Hans and the other sisters, Annemarie and Ida, if she could buy them out so that she would own the house. Hans agreed, and the money from Lotti more than enough covered what we needed for our six months away from home.

With not much time before the start of the school, we packed up our belongings and rented our Manhattan Beach house to a friend. We had prepared ourselves to live in basic accommodations, but upon arrival in Einigen we were pleasantly surprised. The building we stayed in was a beautifully remodeled barn. Our room had a view of Lake Thun, with huge mountains in the background. It was idyllic.

We lived in a community of people from various countries. We received wonderful teaching, did local outreaches, and had our work duties. We learned about hearing God's voice, intercession, and how God provides. What the Lord had taught our children, and what I had seen lived out in their lives, was now confirmed through the DTS teaching. I was humbled to realize that as we had watched our children grow and be obedient to God, we had learned so much through them.

On our outreach following the lecture phase, we took three vans through Eastern Europe to Leningrad (now St. Petersburg), Russia. In cities along the way we worked with local churches and in schools and a prison. We put on open-air outreach events where we sang, danced, and witnessed. One day in Romania we were having a morning prayer meeting, when Rudi Lack, the leader of the school, told me I would be giving my testimony that day.

"Okay," I said. I hoped I looked calm, but inwardly I gulped. Standing and speaking in front of a lot of people did not come naturally to me. I was worried I would dry up or the words wouldn't come out right.

Lord, you have to help me. I can't do this in my own strength, I prayed.

Later that day we prepared for the outreach. A large crowd was forming in the town square, and I tried to ignore my nervousness.

"You'll do great," Hans said reassuringly, giving me a hug.

Suddenly it was my time to speak. *Here we go, Lord. Please give me the words to say,* I prayed silently.

And he did. It took a while to get used to all the people looking and listening to me, and to speak through an interpreter. I am not sure what I said or how long I spoke, but afterward people came forward for prayer and to ask Jesus into their lives. How rewarding!

GUNILA (WITH INTERPRETER) SHARING DURING OUTREACH IN ROMANIA

Later, in a public high school in Oradea, Romania, I walked up to a group of girls and asked, through an interpreter, if I could pray for them. I was overjoyed when each girl said she wanted to become a Christian. Trying to hold back my emotions, I led the girls through a prayer and then hugged them, with tears in my eyes. The Lord had showed me that when I am weak, he is strong.

When our DTS ended, Hans and I returned to California. But we knew it wouldn't be our home for long. Hans was finishing remodeling our house, and then we hoped to sell it and move out of the city to someplace quieter. We heard through our friend Floyd McClung that a YWAM community was being formed in the mountains in a village called Stonewall in southern Colorado. The vision was to buy a large ranch, and then families would buy plots on the ranch and build houses. The ranch would have a training school and community facilities.

"That sounds perfect," I said to Hans. He agreed, and we made plans to move.

We did not move on a whim. God had confirmed that we were heading in the right direction. Being led by the Word of God was a principle we lived by and tried to model to our children. A year earlier we had visited Colorado, and I felt God speak through Joshua 1:3: "I will give you every place where you set your foot

in Switzerland, God s

"advancing into the hil

about his presence goin

With affirmation i

right thing, we sold c

headed to Colorado in

village, God spoke thro

with you, and I will giv

and I know you by nam

Plans changed for

buying, YWAM rented

to the ranch, and Hans l

center for hospitality as

parties, and prayer. They also helped us with projects around the house. With all our children away from home, Hans and I enjoyed our role as "Dad and Mom" to the young people. We had let our children go for the sake of Christ and the gospel, and we were now receiving God's promise in Mark 10:29–30 of gaining many more children.

The land we had purchased was wonderful. Deer, bears, and other wildlife roamed around us, and a river ran through the property. YWAMers would fish for trout, sometimes giving their catch to us for dinner. Surely God had set our boundary in "pleasant places" (Ps. 16:6). I was encouraged by Paul's words: "He determined the times set for them and the exact places where they should live. God did this so that men would seek him and perhaps reach out for him and find him, though he is not far from each one of us. For in him we live and move and have our being" (Acts 17:26–28).

God was reassuring Hans and I not only that he planned the exact places where we would live, but that the same applied for our children. Just as he guided us, he promised to guide them. Knowing that, my heart had peace.

Principles to Live By

- As we release our children to the Lord, he may lead us into similar situations of trusting him, even risky and potentially dangerous circumstances.

- Praying on location where our children have gone to serve the Lord is a privilege and blessing from God.

- As we let our own children go, God is faithful to bring more spiritual children into our homes and lives, to continue the process of blessing and release.

10

WALKING IN OBEDIENCE

I will instruct you and teach you in the way you
should go; I will counsel you and watch over you.
—PSALM 32:8

IT WAS JUST before Christmas in 1987 when Dan walked through the front door of our house in California with a solemn expression on his face. He had just been in a meeting with Pastor Wacker at Calvary Church of the Coastlands. Deep in thought, Dan slowly walked down the hall to his room and shut the door behind him. I decided to leave him alone until he was ready to talk. Just before dinner he came and joined me in the kitchen.

"Is everything okay?" I asked as I sliced tomatoes for a salad.

"Pastor Wacker has offered to have me stay and help here at church instead of going to Afghanistan," he said, taking a seat at the table. He was torn between accepting the offer from his pastor and doing what he felt God had called him to do. He had had the impression from the Lord in his last few weeks at college that he would be sent somewhere for three to six years. Afghanistan was that place.

It would have been tempting for me to agree with Pastor Wacker. After all, Dan would still be serving the Lord by working for the church. And he would be close by. But I knew that such a motivation was selfish. I had to let Dan decide, trusting God that Dan would make the right decision. As Dan's mother, I could emotionally manipulate and try to control the situation, but I knew I had to surrender to God. If he wanted Dan in Afghanistan, then that was the best place for him.

Hans and I talked with Dan later that evening. We discussed how it was important that Dan submit his heart to the Lord while also walk in humility toward Pastor Wacker. But in the end, Dan had to do what he felt the Lord was saying and not live according to the expectations of others. A few days later Dan met Pastor Wacker and turned down the offer to work at the church. His decision was confirmed by peace in his heart. Pastor Wacker was kind and humble and sent Dan off with his blessing.

On September 1, 1988, after seven months in Delhi, Dan flew to Kabul. The drive from the airport to where he would be staying was surreal. Dan felt like he was in a movie. Buildings were bombed out. Army vehicles drove along the streets. Then Dan became aware of background noise—the sound of rockets going off across the city.

The ten-year Soviet War was coming to an end in Afghanistan. The Soviet Union had supported the Marxist

Afghanistan government against the Islamist Mujahideen Resistance. The mujahideen found support from the United States, the United Kingdom, Saudi Arabia, Pakistan, Egypt, and other Muslim nations. The Soviet occupation of Afghanistan had begun on December 24, 1979, and the last troops withdrew in 1989, while Dan was living in the capital.

Despite the war-torn surroundings, Dan lived in comfortable accommodations. He had a maid and a gardener. Few embassies were in the country at that time, and most expats had left because of the intense fighting. Some NGO workers stayed. As a result, many of the larger houses were available to rent quite cheaply. Dan dressed in Western clothes in Kabul to show he was affiliated with the government and not the mujahideen (holy warriors).

It was exciting for us to read Dan's letters about all his new experiences. But not everything was easy for him. When he had arrived in Afghanistan, he was discouraged to find only one other single man on his team—and he was sixty-two years old. There were nineteen single women, but the youngest was still fifteen years older than Dan.

Another challenge was the intensive, four-month language course that Dan was put in. Learning the language didn't come naturally.

"You are the worst student I have ever had, and you will never speak Dari," his teacher said at the end of the course.

"Thanks for your encouragement," Dan replied with a smile. Thankfully this far-from-positive judgment was not true. In time Dan picked up the language.

I was grateful that God was using Dan in the war-torn country. While Dan worked in administration at NOOR Eye

Hospital, he was growing in his love for and dependence on the Lord. His faith was deepening, and many people were being touched by his life.

Dan had befriended a blind Afghan man called Tim at the eye hospital. Tim, who was ten years older than Dan, had become a Christian after traveling to India for an operation and hearing the gospel there. He was now enrolled at a "School for the Blind" connected to the eye hospital. Dan and Tim's friendship grew quickly.

Tim had been persecuted for his faith. The mujahideen had kidnapped him and put him in a tank of water up to his neck for seventy-two hours. If he had fallen asleep, he would have drowned. Amazingly he survived, but not after they had branded his body with a hot iron. The mujahideen were waiting for Tim to deny his faith, but he stood firm. Tim was miraculously rescued when a rocket hit the room next to where he was being held. In the confusion, a man picked Tim up and ran out of the room to safety. Dan was shocked by Tim's story and by the scars up and down his body.

Tim had no fear in sharing about the God who saved his life. One day he was buying a bag of sugar. While carrying the bag, he tripped and fell, and the sugar went everywhere. An old man came to his aid, helping him up and gathering the sugar.

"God has been very bad to you. He has made you live through this war like me, and he has also made you blind," the old man said.

"No, that's not who God is," Tim said. He went on to tell the man about Jesus. They talked for some time. A week later the man and his household of eight gave their lives to Christ.

Dan met with Tim every one or two weeks to support and disciple him. They were careful about how they met because Tim was being watched by three groups: the communist secret police, the mujahideen, and radical Muslims, of whom his uncle was one.

To outsmart his enemies, Tim would meet Dan at a prearranged place in the city, different every time. Dan would pick Tim up on a street corner, and they would drive back to Dan's house, entering through the main gate. Later, Tim would slip out the back gate so as not to arouse suspicion. Dan and Tim would eat together and read the Bible. Dan would pray for his friend and support him in any way he could.

Living in a war zone became normal for Dan. Fifteen to twenty rockets went off each day. A couple of them came within five to ten meters of where Dan was. Dan's life was in danger many times, but God was his protector. While Dan was walking on one side of a concrete wall one day, a rocket hit the other side of the wall. He fell to the ground at the force of the impact but was unhurt. Another time a rocket went off close by, shattering the window above him. Shards of glass fell on his head, but he walked away without a scratch.

When Dan needed to go to the city center for supplies, he would bring an Afghan coworker. One time he and a coworker were taking the hospital's Toyota minivan, and Dan was the passenger. He was feeling tired and decided he would sit and stretch out in one of the back seats with more leg room. As he sat down and was about to close the door, he felt the Holy Spirit say, 'Sit in the front seat." Feeling lazy to move, he was tempted to ignore the prompting, but in obedience he got up and sat in the front passenger seat.

They set off and hadn't gone far when they were sprayed with bullets by a sniper. The bullets went straight through the van and into the back seat. Dan was breathless when he realized where the bullets hit and that God had just saved his life.

Despite this clear protection, at times Dan was afraid and wondered if he should leave the country. He would phone Hans and me and tell us how he was feeling. One time in 1992 he called us, wondering whether he should evacuate with others from the team.

"It's looking pretty bad, Mom. They are telling us we should get out," he said over the crackling line. I told him I would commit to pray with him about what he should do.

I felt the Lord say that Dan should evacuate, but I couldn't get hold of him to tell him. I prayed that he would be able to get out. I didn't hear from him until a few days later.

"I'm in Moscow!" he said.

I was so relieved.

"Where are you going?" I asked. I had sensed in prayer that he should go to Sweden. I laughed when he said that was his destination.

"But, Mom, I don't have any money. I can't buy a ticket," he said.

"Dan, you do have money," I said happily. The day before, he had received two unexpected checks in the mail at home. Together they came to $1,100.

It was an amazing opportunity to partner with my son and to see clearly how God was in control of every step.

Dan explained what had happened up to that point. A group of thirty-five foreigners with children needed to get out of the country because the war was escalating. Dan and his friend John knew the road they would have to take north to the border of Uzbekistan. Commanders of political factions had control of different parts of the road. Dan and the group would be in danger of being kidnapped or having their vehicle taken. So Dan and John went to talk to the commanders to ask for safe passage. They drove north to the city of Mazar-i-Sharif and then turned around and made their way back to Kabul.

As they were passing through the last village before they got back into the city, they were stopped by a group of soldiers. Rolling down the window, Dan answered their questions about who they were and where they were going.

Then one of the soldiers pointed his AK-47 in Dan's direction and said, "We need your car."

"It's not ours. You can't have it," Dan insisted.

Suddenly three soldiers opened the vehicle doors and jumped inside, insisting Dan and John get out.

"We can't," Dan protested, praying that the soldiers would relent.

After half an hour of discussion with the soldiers, the soldiers got out of the car and allowed Dan and John to leave. They sped away as the sun was beginning to set on the horizon. If the predicament had gotten worse, the group of thirty-five would not have been able to evacuate the next day. As it was, Dan believed they should still attempt it.

The group set out early the next morning, praying there would be no incidents on the road. They arrived safely at the Uzbek border. One person in the group spoke Russian and was able to translate and organize visas for the group. After three days, they were all able to fly to Moscow.

Their organization, IAM, paid for all the tickets to Moscow. After that, everyone would return to their home country. On the flight Dan was praying to know where he should go next.

"Go to Sweden," he sensed God speak to his heart. There were several Swedes in the group who would also be going there.

Landing in Moscow Domestic Airport in the middle of the night, the group had to find a way to get to the international airport. They waited at the luggage carousel for their bags, but nothing happened. Time was ticking. It was now about 3:00 a.m., and the group was exhausted. Finally Dan looked through the flaps of the carousel and saw all the luggage from their flight grouped together. The baggage handler saw Dan, whom he recognized as a foreigner, and made a money gesture with his hands. He was looking for a bribe to release the bags.

"This is crazy," Dan muttered. He got another guy from the group, and together they jumped down to where the luggage was. They pushed the man wanting a bribe out of the way and put the bags on the carousel themselves.

Things did not get any easier. As they left the terminal at about 4:30 a.m., they looked for a taxi to the international airport. There was none. Stranded, they wondered what to do.

Not far away they saw a bus. Grabbing their bags, the bedraggled group made their way to it. The driver was sleeping. After waking him, they asked if there was a bus to the airport.

"No," came his groggy reply.

"Where are you going?" Dan asked.

"Nowhere," he said stubbornly, about to close the door. Dan realized this time they should pay, and they offered the driver fifty dollars.

"Come," he said and drove them directly to the airport. They rushed inside and found where to check in for a flight.

Suddenly Dan realized the obvious. "I have no money," he said out loud to himself as he stood in the line to get a flight to Sweden.

"We were wondering what you were going to do," one of the Swedes said behind him.

It was then that Dan phoned home and I told him the good news that God had provided money just in time. One of Dan's friends agreed to pay for his a ticket temporarily, and Dan paid him back after I wired the money to Sweden.

After three weeks in Sweden, when it was safe to return to Afghanistan, Dan traveled back to Kabul.

In August 1993 Dan was helping take eye clinics into the western Himalaya region of Nooristan, made up of five valleys and about half a million people. Only 50 percent of the nation had access to eye doctors, so the clinics were in demand. The team drove for two days and set out hiking for another two days to get to their destination. They would camp for two weeks and treat about 150 patients a day.

Halfway through the first day of hiking, Dan found himself at the back of the line and out of view of the rest of the team who had turned a corner. The rock trail was steep and covered with loose sand. Dan slipped and fell and began to slide down the rock. At first he wasn't worried, until he realized he was heading for the edge of a cliff—a one-thousand-foot drop into a dry river bed. As Dan slid, he tried to grab on to something, but there was nothing to grab.

"Help!" he shouted. But his cries went unheard. The group had already moved ahead.

At the cliff's edge, Dan saw a few blades of grass sticking out of the rock. In desperation he cried out "Jesus!" and clutched the grass. Amazingly it held, and Dan's feet swung like a pendulum over the edge. Quickly scanning the rock face for anything else to hang on to, Dan spotted a crack and wedged his hands into it. As he got a safer hold, he saw another crack, and slowly he was able to pull himself up to safety. Shaken, he ran to tell the others what had happened.

Three years later Dan was at a YWAM conference in Colorado Springs and was catching up with a friend from Brazil.

"Did anything happen to you three years ago?" she asked.

Dan smiled curiously at the unusual question. "I don't think so."

She persisted. "Try to remember, Dan. Did anything happened to you in August 1993?"

Then Dan remembered the cliff incident and explained to her what happened. His friend said that God had woken her up in the night to pray for Dan's protection because his life was in danger and that she obeyed. She showed Dan her prayer journal, and they confirmed that she had been praying at the exact time that Dan's life was saved by a few blades of grass.

I was astounded when I heard this story. It fed my faith and reminded me that God is in control and that he can take care of my children. Dan was learning to ask the Lord, moment by moment, for instructions, in small details and in dangerous situations. The Lord was counseling him and watching over him. Hans and I joined Dan in giving glory to God for his great favor and blessing.

Principles to Live By

- We need to trust God that our children will follow his purposes, whatever and wherever that means. We must avoid the temptation to emotionally manipulate our children.

- We can trust God in all the situations our children face. He will do the extraordinary, like wake people up at night to pray for our children's safety.

11

PEACE IN THE VALLEY

Show me your ways, O LORD, teach me your paths.
—PSALM 25:4

WHILE CHRISTINA was attending the School of Biblical Studies in Hong Kong, we started hearing more and more from her about a young Canadian man named Greg.

"I wonder if something will come of this," I mused to Hans after reading one of Christina's letters. Christina had started a prayer group with Greg to intercede for different parts of the world. It was while praying for others that they began to fall in love.

After the school in Hong Kong, Christina moved back to New Delhi and a year later moved to Honolulu to staff the YWAM base there. Greg went home to work in Canada for a few months, and then moved to Honolulu also. Christina and Greg's time apart had confirmed their feelings for each other, and on June 5, 1991, Greg proposed. The wedding was planned for November of that year in Honolulu. Hans and I were excited for our daughter as she embarked on this new journey. The ceremony was held in a nearby church, which Christina's friends had decorated with beautiful Hawaiian flowers. The reception was held at the Diamond Head Hilton, where they were engaged.

CHRISTINA & GREG, HONOLULU 1991

Greg and Christina sought the Lord for direction in their new life together. They felt led to help pioneer a work in Thailand for two years. They would then set their sights on India.

One afternoon they went to grab a drink at Manoa Coffee near the YWAM base in Honolulu. There they discussed their options. They had heard Greg Dennington, a YWAM leader in Taiwan, speaking about what the first two years in pioneer ministry might look like, and his words had caused them to rethink their plans.

"Why are we going to Thailand? All that effort learning the language, and then we leave for India," Christina said. Greg agreed that somehow it didn't make sense. They decided they would pray with their friends Bruce and Lisa Burchfield, hoping for a word of direction from the Lord.

A few hours later the four of them sat down on the sofas in the Burchfields' small wooden house on the YWAM base and started to pray. After a while, they stopped and asked each other what they had felt the Lord say. They came away with three things: Muslim, northwest India, and mountain. The latter was prompted by the words of Psalm 121:1, "I lift up my eyes to the hills."

"Lord, please show us what to do with this. Open a door for us," Greg prayed.

Later that day Bruce went to the consulate in Honolulu. He noticed a leaflet and brought it to Greg and Christina. It was an advertisement for Queen of the Hills, a hill station in Mussoorie, northwestern India, picturing beautiful mountains behind a lush valley. On the front of the brochure were the words "I lift up my eyes to the hills." Christina and Greg saw this as a confirmation of what they had received in prayer. Later they found out there was a language school in Mussoorie. Since India was where Greg and Christina believed they would serve long-term, it made sense to learn the language in India. So they inquired about becoming students there.

With a new sense of direction the newly married couple set off in March 1993 for New Delhi, India, on their way to Mussoorie in the Himalayas. Greg's parents traveled with them from Thailand to India. The journey from New Delhi to Mussoorie took twelve hours on a road snaking up to seven thousand feet in the foothills.

For the first couple of nights Greg and Christina would be staying at the Shilton Hotel. A far cry from the Hilton, the hotel had no windows and smelled musty. It was wet and foggy when they arrived late at night. They had a quick meal and tried to get comfortable in the lumpy bed, hoping for a good night's sleep.

The next morning, aching from the uncomfortable mattress, they set out to look for a new home. On their walk they met some other missionaries, an old Canadian woman named Julia and a Korean family who were serving with YWAM.

"Be careful whom you speak to. Watch out for the Communist party leaders," Julia warned.

Greg and Christina thanked her for her timely advice. One of the Communist leaders had already contacted Greg and Christina, offering to help. They didn't know whether to trust him, but now they knew they should be careful.

When the Korean family and their baby twins invited Greg and Christina to stay with them until they found something more permanent, they readily agreed. The first night, as they sank into a warm bed, feeling the heat of the Korean electric blanket, they thanked God for his protection and provision.

Soon they found their own place to live and started their eight hours of daily language study, trying to master Hindustani. After six months Greg and Christina were joined by a small team: Bruce and Lisa Burchfield and Melissa Shepardson, a close friend of Christina's.

While learning the language, Greg and Christina asked God to direct their next steps. They had to find the Muslims that God had spoken to them about. But the majority of people in Mussoorie were Hindu, and information on people and language groups in the area was hard to come by. So Greg and Christina decided to do a survey themselves and find out who their neighbors were. They took a bus into surrounding villages to scout out the land. When they arrived at the hill station of Shimla, they found almost five thousand Kashmiri Muslims. But they were all men looking for work and were without their families.

Wanting to work with Muslim men and women, Greg and Christina moved on. They rode a bus through the night to Chamba, an eighteen-hour journey sitting on wooden benches. By the time they arrived their bodies were aching. In Chamba they met a small group of nomadic Muslim shepherds.

"Lord, where are the Muslims you told us about?" they prayed.

They felt a challenge in reply: "Why are you not considering Kashmir?"

At that time the area between India and Pakistan was very dangerous. Kashmir is divided into three regions—Jammu, the Kashmir Valley, and Ladakh—each of which is dominated by a different ethnic group. Jammu is inhabited by a Hindu majority, the Kashmir Valley by a Muslim majority, and Ladakh by a Buddhist majority.

Christina prayed, "We know we cannot let fear be the basis of our decision, but we ask, Lord, that you would make it clear if we are to go to Kashmir."

Each member of the team felt a peace to go ahead. Christina was excited. Ever since her outreach to the area, she had a love for the people and a desire to work with them. Greg, Christina, Bruce, and Melissa set off for Amritsar, a holy city in the Sikh faith, to catch a flight to Kashmir. Lisa stayed in Mussoorie with their three kids—Joshua, Brandon, and little Jessica, who has just turned one.

"Do you have any money?" Christina asked Greg after a couple of hours in the taxi to Amritsar. He didn't. In fact, none of them had any money.

The taxi driver wanted to stop on the hour, every hour, to drink chai, but when they explained they needed to get to the bank before it closed, he kept going. They arrived in Amritsar minutes before the banks closed for the day.

Rushing into the building, they found that the bank teller would need to call Bombay to authorize their credit card for cash, but the phone lines were down.

"Lord, we need you right now," Christina prayed quietly.

"Try the phones again," Greg suggested to the bank teller.

This time they worked, and Bombay gave authorization. They drove to the airport, paid the taxi driver, and bought tickets to the city of Srinagar in Kashmir. Melissa felt led by God not to continue to Kashmir but to go back to Mussoorie and wait for the team. Greg, Christina, and Bruce said goodbye to Melissa and made their way to their plane.

"Looks like we are the only passengers," Bruce said, smiling.

Only three other passengers boarded. No one wanted to go to Srinagar. Unknown to the group, Kashmir was in the middle of a *hartal*, or curfew. Because of fighting, the people of Srinagar had not been able to leave their homes to get food.

They had been stuck inside for eighteen days, unable to live normal daily lives.

Despite not knowing about this latest turn of events, Greg and Christina had learned about the history of the area. In the late fourteenth century, after years of Buddhist and Hindu rule, Kashmir was conquered by Muslims and later became part of the Mughal Empire. In the mid-nineteenth century the British purchased Kashmir and installed a Hindu prince as ruler of the predominantly Muslim region. When India declared independence in 1947, Muslim forces from Pakistan invaded Kashmir. The Hindu ruler fled to Delhi and agreed to place Kashmir under the dominion of India. Indian troops flew to Srinagar to engage the Pakistani forces. The fighting was ended by a UN cease-fire in 1949, but the region was divided between India and Pakistan along the cease-fire line. In the late 1980s, Muslim resistance to Indian rule escalated, with some militants supporting independence, and others union with Pakistan. Plans to hold elections in 1995 were abandoned following the burning of an important Muslim shrine and its surrounding town and riots in Srinagar.

It was with this in mind that Greg and Christina landed at the airport in Srinagar. The plane taxied to a halt. Outside was a white blanket of freshly fallen snow. A cease-fire had just been called that day, and the curfew was lifted temporarily, enabling the group to leave the airport safely. As they walked outside with their suitcases into the cold air, they were bombarded by taxi drivers vying for business. One bold driver snatched their bags and placed them in his car. There was little they could do but follow.

He drove them through streets, informing them that Muslim militants were hiding out in a holy shrine, fighting against the Indian army. The city looked very much like it was in the middle of a war. Army bunkers lined the empty streets, and tension filled the air. The group decided to keep a low profile and find out more about what was going on. At their hotel they warmed up by the wooden stove, and they were each given a hot water bottle for their beds to keep warm as they slept.

The next day Christina, Greg, and Bruce made their way outside. People were scurrying about, trying to get food while the curfew was lifted. Many wore long ponchos called *ferhans* that went below their knees. To keep warm, they pulled their arms inside and carried a clay pot in a wicker basket (*kangri*) with hot coal inside. Christina laughed, as the bulge under the poncho made people, even the men, look heavily pregnant. The pots are locally referred to as a "winter-wife." The people in this Islamic culture dressed very differently from their Indian brothers and sisters to the south.

That evening, after spending the day praying as they walked the streets, Greg, Christina, and Bruce sat down for a meal with delicious mild curry and rice with curds. As they sat and talked, they recognized the peace they had. Although it didn't make outward sense given the circumstances, they knew that they could live in Srinagar. And they wanted to live there. The Kashmiri people were so friendly and grateful that they had not been forgotten by the outside world.

By the end of three days the group headed to the airport to catch a plane back home. The day they left, the cease-fire was lifted and fighting resumed. The only days it had stopped were the three days Greg, Christina, and Bruce were in the city. God had surely been watching over them.

Back in Mussoorie they continued to pray for direction. A couple of days after the trip to Kashmir, Greg glanced at a calendar on the wall. It had a picture of a beautiful valley with the words "Even though I walk through the valley, I will not fear." Srinagar was in a valley, and Greg knew God was speaking into his heart that they need not fear.

Greg, Christina, Bruce, Lisa, and the children made plans to move to Kashmir. In February 1995 they flew into Srinagar and saw the huge mountains surrounding the valley. The mountains had protected the culture of the people in the valley, but it had also kept them isolated. It was a daunting prospect to live in such an isolated mountainous place. But God spoke again of his presence with them. "Don't see the mountains as forcing your isolation. Look at them as a picture of my greatness and remember what I have done," he said.

With peace in their hearts, Greg and Christina and their team settled in Srinagar to bring the gospel to the Kashmiri Muslims. Right after they arrived, they stayed with Bruce and Lisa in a rented house with little furniture and no heat. Shivering from the freezing weather, they huddled in one room with their fire pots (*kangris*), talking and praying. Bruce and Lisa's luggage was being sent up on a truck from Delhi. There had been a landslide on the road, and the truck was stuck somewhere along the 800-kilometer (500-mile) route.

Their new life was certainly different from the relative peace of the United State. Stories of nearby gunfights and exploding land mines were common. When the weather was warmer, Greg and Christina would lie on the grass at night and watch the tracers in the sky from the rapid fire. They often drove through the narrow alleyways lined with Indian army men searching for militants hidden in residential homes. One time there was exchange of gunfire as Greg was driving down an alley. A young Kashmiri man standing at a doorway waved his hand to show him which way to go to avoid the gunfire, and Greg veered off in a safe direction.

When Greg and Christina had been preparing to move, Greg got a call asking to help a Shia Muslim family move from Delhi back to Srinagar. He agreed to help the family move. Once in Srinagar, the family invited Greg and Christina to live with them in the Old City. Greg and Christina decided it would be a perfect opportunity to get to know the culture and the people. They accepted the invitation and were instantly adopted by the family, welcomed unreservedly into their home. When Greg asked to borrow the family car to run an errand, the father replied firmly, "Why do you ask me? You are my son. All I have is yours. You never need to ask again."

In the fall of 1995, Hans and I traveled to India to see firsthand where our children were living. We stayed with Elisabeth and Steve in Pune for two months, helping to look after their little girl Carin while they staffed a Leadership Training School. Carin had been born in May 1994, and it was a joy to be with our first grandchild. Christina and Greg also came to the school in Pune, and for two months we were together as a family. Even Dan was able to come for a few days.

After the school ended in December, we flew to Kashmir with Greg, Christina, and their friend Sara, a fellow YWAMer in her late twenties. "We're home," Greg said as we stepped onto the tarmac.

When we arrived at the home of Deborah and Hassan, the Muslim family Greg and Christina lived with, they greeted us with arms outstretched and shouts of joy. It was obvious to me that they had missed Greg and Christina. I was comforted seeing how much they loved my daughter and her husband. Even though the city was in a state of war, Greg and Christina's home life was stable and they were looked after.

CHRISTINA & GREG IN KASHMIR

Deborah and Hassan's house was very simple. Electricity was intermittent, and only one room was heated. Outside it was just above freezing, and we gratefully received our bedtime hot water bottles from their fifteen-year-old servant boy.

Hans was not feeling well when we arrived and spent a lot of time sleeping. He stayed behind when we went to visit Hassan's business, a carpet and souvenir shop. As we drove through the town, the fighting seemed close, but people were trying to get on with business as usual. Indian soldiers were constantly patrolling the streets or were hunkering behind sand bags along the road, ready to shoot at any sign of insurgents. The next day we stayed close to home because there was a general strike and curfew. The sky was overcast, electricity was off, and an atmosphere of tension permeated the city. As we walked the streets near home, we saw an eighty-year-old man painting papier-mâché boxes, a specialty craft of the area. I marveled at the beauty of his creations and at the man's peaceful work of intricate painting amid such turbulent times.

Another day we visited the only church in the area, St. Andrews. The pastor was from Ladahk and had endured much persecution. The building had been burned down twice, once in 1967 and again in 1979. But the pastor was now seeing fruit and had baptized a new believer the previous week.

One morning at Hassan and Deborah's home, we had a prayer time in the main room, and our hosts joined us. Hassan prayed while Deborah just observed. Through this I saw the impact of Greg and Christina sharing their lives with this lovely family. Doors were opened to them that could not have been opened any other way. Each evening fifteen to twenty family and friends of Hassan and Deborah would join us to eat. Greg and Christina, who were treated as adopted children, had constant opportunities to talk about their faith. Deborah and Hassan brought the people to them. Greg and Christina gave copies of the Bible to seven men who were reading through it.

After a few days Sara, who had come with us hoping to work in Kashmir some day, was flying back to the United States. A couple of hours after leaving for the airport, Greg, Hassan, and Sara returned because her flight had been canceled. Minutes before they came back through the door, we had heard shooting. We found out later that nine militants had been killed in an area they had just passed through. We praised God that he had kept them safe.

Our week in Srinagar went by fast, and Hans was feeling better. He had been treated with such respect by the family. They sat on cushions on the floor, but Hans found it difficult to bend down because of his sore knees. With much ceremony Hassan brought out one of the few chairs they had so that Hans could sit with us. Sitting in the chair, he looked like the patriarch of the family.

We said our good-byes and hugged Deborah and Hassan with tears in our eyes. They had been so warm and welcoming to us. Sara was coming with us to the airport to try to get on a flight. As we drove through the street where the shootings had been, we saw lots of people milling around and waiting to see if anything would kick off again. I prayed that Greg and Christina would be safe on their drive back.

We passed two checkpoints on our way to the airport. At each one we had to get out of the car and were body searched. It helped that Greg could speak the language. As we neared the airport, Sara realized that she had left part of her ticket at Deborah and Hassan's house. But if we turned back, we would miss our flight. Together we asked God to intervene. As we were praying, he was answering our prayers. Back at the house Deborah had noticed the documents lying on a table. Quickly, she dispatched the servant boy to take them to the airport. He arrived just in time and ran up to us with a big grin.

Checking in, Sara was told that over ninety people were on the waiting list for a flight and that she would never get on. Again, we prayed, and Greg also spoke to the flight attendants.

Sara not only got on the flight, but she was bumped up to business class. We all laughed and praised the God who makes a way where there seems to be no way.

Hugging Greg and Christina good-bye, I was thankful that God had chosen them to be hope and peace to one Shia family in Srinagar. They were also a light in the city, paving the way and keeping the door open for other Christians to come in the future. I saw the dangers, but I knew in my heart that the safest place to be was in the center of God's will. That was where Greg and Christina, as well as Hans and I, were experiencing the Lord's promised peace.

Living in the realities of a war-torn country was very different from my home life in Colorado. But seeing where my children and grandchildren lived, and meeting in person those they talked about, fueled my prayers. If it wasn't enough to have a daughter living in an unstable area, Dan was about to go into Iran, a country that did not welcome Christian missionaries.

Principles to Live By

- God will nudge us to pray for our children. Even if we do not know what they are facing, God does, and we can trust him.

- Interceding for our children and the nations they work in helps to dispel our natural worries and fears.

12

TRUSTING IN GOD'S PURPOSES

The LORD is my rock, my fortress and my deliverer;
my God is my rock, in whom I take refuge. He is my
shield and the horn of my salvation, my stronghold.
—PSALM 18:2

THE COLD Colorado winter was breathtakingly beautiful. Snow decorated the fir trees and the Sangre de Cristo Mountains. It was 1997, and Hans was finishing up work on our log house. In the meantime we were living in a ten-by-twenty-foot room at the back of our garage on the property.

As Hans and I celebrated the New Year together in Stonewall, Colorado, we wondered what 1997 would bring. "Let all the children be kept safe and be blessed this coming year," was my prayer for them. A few days later, on January 5, I wrote in my prayer journal, "May your purpose be accomplished in me this year—what you purposed before the foundation of the world. Let me be teachable, faithful, flexible, honest, holy, and pure!"

The girls and their husbands were in India. Christina and Greg would be traveling back to Canada shortly for the birth of their first child. Elisabeth and Steve had two girls by this time, Carin and Annalisa, who was born in June 1996. Dan was living in Turkmenistan. Just before the New Year, on December 26, he left on a two-week trip to Iran to make contacts and find ways to share the gospel. We were praying for him, and it sounded like he would be having a great time.

On January 8 I sat down for lunch with Hans. "Dan should be home from Iran by now," I commented, remembering that it had been two weeks since he left Turkmenistan. I was surprised we hadn't heard from him. On the eleventh Dan was supposed to travel to London to visit a friend, but we still hadn't heard from him. On the sixteenth we got news from Dan's coworkers in Turkmenistan that Glenn Murray, the South African friend Dan had traveled with, had been detained in Iran. They had taken his passport at the border, saying they found irregularities. But we still had no word about Dan. I started to get concerned.

Not knowing what had happened was the hardest part. We were eagerly waiting for news about our son. Because Hans was Swiss, all our children had Swiss passports in addition to American passports. There was no American embassy in Tehran at that time, so Switzerland helped to handle American interests. Hans contacted the Swiss Embassy in Tehran by fax to ask for any information and to let them know that Dan was missing.

On January 18 we received word about Dan from the Swiss embassy in Tehran. He was alive but was also detained.

He had traveled using his Swiss passport, and the guards had taken it at the border when he was returning to Turkmenistan. As with Glenn's passport, they said they had found irregularities. Both Dan and Glenn had been sent to Tehran to resolve their passport issues but instead were interrogated and put in Evin Prison in the city.

Immediately upon hearing the news, we contacted YWAMers and friends all over the world to pray. We phoned Elisabeth and Steve in India. As part of our family and also YWAM's international leadership, they were very concerned. There was a real chance Dan could be executed for being an assumed CIA spy or for being a Christian and sharing his faith.

"Lord, keep Dan and Glenn in your care. Give them wisdom, boldness, peace, and joy. And bring them back safely," was the constant prayer on my lips. But I was so busy organizing prayer, contacting government offices, and making phone calls, I hardly had time to process that my son was in prison and that his life was in danger.

As I was walking over to the YWAM office to copy a fax, I encountered Floyd McClung, who was out for a walk. He lived next door to us and knew all the details about Dan.

"Gunila, how are you?" he asked with concern in his eyes.

A rush of emotion came over me. All the tension and anxiety that had been building up suddenly broke over the banks. I burst into tears. Floyd, in his loving, fatherly way, prayed for me and for Dan. My tension began to ease, and by the time I got to the office, I felt more at peace.

Over the next few days we received responses from people around the world. I clung to the words of encouragement and was moved to tears when I heard of people praying and fasting for Dan. Our former church, Calvary Church of the Coastlands, had dedicated an entire service to pray for Dan's safety. Isaiah 54:17 came up again and again—that no weapon formed against Dan would prosper. We prayed that would be the case.

Day after day went by, and no good news about Dan came. The Swiss embassy was keeping us informed, but they hadn't been allowed to visit Dan in prison. Glenn, on the other hand, had met with the South African officials, and it was confirmed that he was okay but still in prison.

By this time Floyd McClung and the base had established a daily routine of prayer and fasting for Dan. I met with a few others at one meeting. In my heart I trusted God, and I had released Dan into his hands. I knew God had a purpose in this. "Father, don't release Dan until your purposes are fulfilled," I prayed from my heart, tears spilling down my face.

Still, the fearful thought tried to crowd my mind: "Is he alive or dead?" The only way to combat this was to recall all I knew about God's character and to read the Bible and pray. I built up my faith by reciting his Word, summarizing passages like Psalm 145: "The Lord is great, worthy of praise, majestic, abundant in goodness. I will joyfully sing of his righteousness. He is gracious, compassionate, slow to anger, rich in love, mighty, faithful to all his promises, fulfilling the desires of whose who fear him." As I kept on remembering who God was, my eyes would be lifted to him, and I would find peace in trusting a God who is all powerful, all knowing, and all present. I chose to fix my eyes on Jesus, not on the circumstances—a choice I had to repeat over and over again.

On January 23 I started a three-day fast for Dan. We had been told it was best not to make Dan's imprisonment public news, as it could jeopardize his position if he was still alive. On the twenty-eighth we had news from the Swiss Ambassador in Tehran that they had not been able to contact Dan and had been refused permission to see him. It was only God's grace that upheld us at that time. Hans and I could do nothing more but trust in our heavenly Father and his character.

By February 6 the snowy scenery in Stonewall was as picturesque as ever. After my morning prayers I took a walk outside in the fresh air.

"Gunila, a fax just arrived. It's from Dan," Hans shouted when I returned.

My heart started beating fast. As I held the fax in my hands, tears of relief gushed from my eyes. I recognized Dan's handwriting. Our son was alive! In just a few lines he said he was all right, but there were no details. Hans and I thanked the Lord that we had contact.

My Bible reading for the day had been from 2 Kings 19. King Hezekiah received a letter and spread it before the Lord, praying: "O Lord, God of Israel, enthroned between the cherubim, you alone are God over all the kingdoms of the earth. . . . Give ear, O Lord, and hear; open your eyes, O Lord, and see" (vv. 15–16). I did the same with my letter, spreading it on the floor and praying the prayer of Hezekiah with all my heart.

A few days passed with not much news from Iran, but I felt encouraged in the Lord. I believed God was working behind the scenes, even though I couldn't see it. Hans had offered to fly to Iran, but we had been told it was better to work through the diplomatic channels.

Then news came that Glenn had been released from prison. We were overjoyed. I phoned Glenn's mother in South

Africa, laughing with her and understanding her tears of joy. The YWAM base held an evening of praise and celebration. We thanked God that Glenn was free, and we felt encouraged that Dan would be released soon also.

The next day we had more good news. Dan had been allowed a visit from the Swiss embassy. And not only that, but that day we also became the proud grandparents of our first grandson. Christina gave birth to a little boy, whom she and Greg named Caleb Daniel, after his uncle who was currently incarcerated in Iran. While I was relieved to know that the Swiss embassy had reached Dan, I was also concerned when the embassy said Dan seemed depressed. I prayed for hope to rise up in him.

At this point we were advised to go public with the news. We sent out a press release on February 24. As soon as the news was out, the phones were ringing nonstop. We were contacted by news agencies from around the world. The Swedish newspaper *Dagen* even ran the story on their front page.

Amid all the activity, Hans celebrated his seventieth birthday on March 1, 1997. Two days later he began to feel sick. He was coughing and having difficulty breathing.

"We'd better get you to the hospital," I said, worried by how pale and weak he looked. Hans suffered from congestive heart failure, and the stress of Dan in prison had complicated his illness.

Lord, heal him, I prayed silently as we drove to the hospital.

Hans was admitted to the hospital, and his health began to improve. After a couple of days, I brought him home. Though there had been no more news about Dan, I was relieved to have my husband back.

On March 11 the Iranian ambassador in Switzerland flew to Iran to talk with the president of Iran, Akbar Hashemi Rafsanjani, about Dan's imprisonment. The situation was being dealt with through the highest possible channels.

The next day Hans and I were eating breakfast when the phone rang. It was good news from the Swiss embassy. Dan might be released in a week, they told us. There was no guarantee, but things looked hopeful. We learned that the Iranian authorities had doubted that Dan was Swiss because he didn't speak the language. They thought he was a CIA spy who had stolen a Swiss passport. But when the Iranian authorities heard Hans speaking on the phone in Swiss German with the Swiss embassy in Tehran—all the lines were tapped—they started to believe Dan might be telling the truth.

Hans and I rejoiced at the news, quickly passing it on to others for prayer. We also asked our supporters to keep it quiet because things could change in an instant, and we didn't want to exacerbate the situation with the Iranian government.

Later that day I met with some YWAMers to pray. "Lord, let nothing hinder this release process," I prayed with all my heart. In faith Hans and I prepared for Dan's release. We learned about Le Rucher, a ministry in Geneva that works with people who have come out of traumatic situations.

A few days later we awoke to a breathtakingly beautiful day. The morning fog had frozen on the trees, causing a fairytale-like pattern to surround the house. The sun was shining in the clear blue sky, bluebirds and robins were chirping, the snow had melted, and plants were rising from the earth. Spring was on its way. Change was coming. In winter everything seems dead, but slowly as the sun starts to warm things up, the growth going on underground comes to life. I prayed the same for Dan's situation—that the invisible work God had been doing would now come to light. In my heart I had a peace about Dan. God was in control.

That night we went to bed, turning the light out after praying for Dan. At 1:30 a.m. the phone rang. I woke up startled.

"Hello," I said groggily, lifting the receiver to my ear.

"Mom, it's me. I'm free," Dan shouted over the phone.

"Dan!" I breathed, hoping that this was real and not a dream. "Thank the Lord you are free!" I laughed and cried tears of joy at the same time.

Hans took the phone and got some details from Dan. He was still in Iran, staying at the Swiss embassy. They were in the process of organizing his flight out of the country to Switzerland.

When Hans put the phone down, we both jumped up and down for joy. Arms in the air, we praised the Lord that our boy was alive and free. We quickly spread the news, and friends in different time zones around the world started calling straightaway. I spoke to Glenn in South Africa. He was overjoyed to hear the news and arranged to meet us with his mother in Switzerland in a few days.

As soon as the sun came up and the business day commenced, I called to book two flights to Zurich. Hans and I had enough air miles for free tickets.

"I am sorry, but if you want to use your air miles, you need to book two weeks in advance," the woman said.

My heart sank. We wanted to leave the next day, and to pay the full price of the tickets was very expensive. We didn't have that kind of money.

Lord, help, I cried out silently.

I explained to the woman the circumstances of our situation. "Our son is being released from prison in Iran, and we need to meet him in Switzerland," I said.

The woman went to speak with her supervisor. I waited, hoping against hope that they would be kind. They were. We were given special dispensation, and we were able to pay for tickets for the next day in full with air miles.

As Hans and I sat holding hands on the flight from Colorado Springs to Zurich, we breathed deeply, hardly able to take in all that had happened over the last nine weeks. It had been a huge test in trusting God. But because we had already released Dan to God and his work, when a situation as serious as this arose, we were able to put into practice what we had learned over the years.

Several times the Lord had spoken to me about Dan from Jeremiah 1. I believed Dan, like Jeremiah, was known by God and set apart before he was born. He was appointed as a prophet to the nations, and I felt God was saying to Dan, "Do not be afraid. I am with you and will rescue you. Stand up and say to them whatever I command you. Do not be terrified by them." I found out later that Dan had spoken only the truth when questioned by a judge. He was asked why he was in Iran. Dan replied that he wanted to find out ways in which he could tell the Iranian people about Christ. Saying this could have led to his death, but he was miraculously spared. Truly, God had been faithful to his character.

At about the same time as Dan was being questioned, I was encouraged by reading Ezra 1:1–3: "The LORD moved the heart of Cyrus king of Persia" to let his people go. I had been praying that God would move the hearts of the authorities in Iran and release my son.

After all the prayer and trusting God, it seemed like a dream that we would actually be seeing Dan face to face very soon. Coming out of customs at Zurich Airport, we saw Dan walking to meet us. He had flown in the day before and was staying with Hans's sister Lotti.

"Dan!" I cried, running to him. He had lost a lot of weight and had grown a thick beard and long hair while in prison—but now he was *free,* and we were seeing him *alive!*

Dan, Hans, and I hugged each other close in the middle of the bustling airport. People were rushing by, but we were oblivious, completely overjoyed at being together again. Lotti joined us, and we made our way to the car.

There was so much to talk about. Dan was in good spirits, but it shook me to hear how depressed he had become in prison, even attempting suicide. We ate at McDonald's— Dan's decision—and he told us more about his experience. Three of the guards had become Christians while Dan was imprisoned. I cried as I heard this. My son's sacrifice of freedom became an instrument for the guards' salvation. Now God had mercifully set Dan free.

During our time in Switzerland, we went to Le Rucher, whose facility is just across the border in France, for some sessions. Dan found them very helpful to process all that had happened. We visited the United Nations in Geneva and met Jean-Daniel Vigry who had worked on Dan's case at the UNHCR, the UN refugee agency. In Bern, Switzerland, we stopped for debriefing at the American embassy, and Dan was issued a new passport because his American passport had expired while in prison. He had to use his American passport to leave or enter the United States but could use his Swiss passport between countries outside the United States.

A few days later was Easter. With Hans's family we feasted and went on a beautiful hike in the Alps. As the sun began to set, we had our own Easter service and proclaimed, "Christ is alive and risen indeed!"

Principles to Live By

- There are very real "dark valleys"—whether physical, mental, or emotional—that we walk through with our children. Having released them into God's hands, we know he has purposes in both joys and trials.

- Rehearsing all we know about God's character builds up our faith as we face difficult times with our children.

- We must fix our eyes on Jesus and not on the circumstances—a choice to be repeated again and again.

13

REUNION IN
SWITZERLAND

*May the LORD bless you from Zion all the days of your
life; may you see the prosperity of Jerusalem, and may you
live to see your children's children. Peace be upon Israel.*
—PSALM 128:5–6

IN 2001 it had been several years since our entire family
had all been together. Hans had been talking about a family
reunion in Switzerland, and the time seemed right. Our children were excited at the prospect of being together in their
father's homeland. In June, Dan and the girls, with families,
flew to Switzerland to join me, Hans, and Lottie. We stayed
at an old farmhouse built in 1689 where Hans had gone to
children's camp as a young boy. The view at Lake Walen, with
the Churfirsten Mountains in the background, was picture-
book beautiful.

On the first evening that the twelve of us sat around the
large wooden table, my heart soared with pride. Everyone was

laughing and joking, telling stories, and reminiscing over the past few years. Dan's first book, *Imprisoned in Iran,* had come out, and each of us talked about those frightening weeks of not knowing Dan's fate.

FAMILY REUNION IN SWITZERLAND, 2001

Dan had joined us from Iraq, where he had been invited to be part of a delegation of three hundred people working to stop sanctions against the country. He had been touched by the trip, traveling to the locations of the biblical cities of Ur, Babylon, and Nineveh. His heart broke as he drove through the desert and saw the Bedouin and other travelers who needed to hear the Good News. Being in that part of the world also meant that Dan had to deal with fears resurfacing from his prison experience. God gave him victory and a peace that he was with him.

Before the trip to Iraq, Dan had been traveling with Loren Cunningham, the founder of YWAM. Dan spoke alongside Loren at different engagements. It was a privilege for Dan, reaffirming his desire to not only go to hard places but also encourage young people to be obedient to God and walk closely with him. We were grateful for Dan's many connections. He was able to borrow a van from friends in Germany, which enabled our whole family to go sightseeing together.

Steve and Elisabeth were in good health. They were excited about what God was doing in India. Steve had just been given the job as director of YWAM's International Frontier Missions, and together Steve and Lis were directors of YWAM in South and Central Asia. Elisabeth was the director of University of the Nations in India, which had trained hundreds of workers and started many projects and churches.

Their daughters, seven-year-old Carin and five-year-old Annalisa, knew India as their home. Annalisa was intrigued by the animals on the neighboring farm. They were nothing unusual, just goats and sheep. But to a little girl who was used to elephants and camels, they were very interesting.

Looking at Carin, so full of life, I recalled the fearful and life-threatening circumstances of her birth. In 1993 Elisabeth was in Tonga for a Leadership Training School. While Carin was in her womb, she traveled to eleven countries, carrying out her responsibilities. Five months into the pregnancy she developed toxemia, which causes high blood pressure and was dangerous for both Elisabeth and the baby. Later she was ordered full bed rest by the doctor.

Back home in Pune, seven weeks before her due date, Lis had an appointment with the doctor. Steve took her to the appointment. When they arrived, the doctor found that Lis's blood pressure was 220/170, compared to the normal 120/80. "We need to deliver this baby right away," she told Steve.

Elisabeth was rushed into the delivery room, and Carin was born by cesarean section, weighing only three pounds, four ounces. On the second day after the birth, a pediatrician took Lis and Steve aside. He said that because of her low birthweight, their daughter might not survive. Devastated and afraid, they called us to start praying for a miracle. God moved on our behalf, and after three weeks in intensive care Carin was strong enough, at five pounds, to go home.

A few months after this experience, Elisabeth, Steve, and Carin were in Bangladesh, where tiny Carin contracted pneumonia. They had to fly to Dakka to get Carin to a hospital. It was monsoon season, and they flew through a dramatic storm. Lis was terrified, wondering if the little plane would make it. Right then she realized her helplessness; there was nothing she could do but trust God. Sitting in the plane, she came to a place of complete surrender to God for her daughter, her husband, and herself. At that moment she felt her spirit was set free from fear.

They landed safely and went straight to the hospital, where Carin received antibiotics. After five days in the hospital God spoke to Lis as she watched her daughter get better.

"You can trust me," he said.

Lis had peace. Despite the circumstances, she knew deep down that God was trustworthy.

When Carin was well again, they traveled to Calcutta and visited Mother Teresa's orphanage, participating in the Roman

Catholic Mass. As Mother Teresa walked past, she saw Carin and asked to pick her up. The saintly nun held baby Carin in her arms and prayed over her life. Lis and Steve were deeply touched, and they took a photograph for Carin to see when she was older. Now, as I looked at Carin running around in the sun or reading with her head in a book, it was hard to believe that she had to fight for her life. God had completely restored her.

I was reminded of times when I had seen God's healing power in the lives of our children. In 1989, when Christina arrived in Hong Kong for the School of Biblical Studies before moving back to India, she was suffering from stomach pain. It was so severe that after a few days on the base she had to go to the hospital. The doctor told her she had a kidney infection. Wanting a second opinion, the next day Christina went with a leader from the base to another doctor, who confirmed the diagnosis. She was able to get the right medicine, and the Lord restored her.

In 1982 Elisabeth was in Calcutta. During a reporting time with teams in the area, she started to feel feverish. The team was staying in an old British mission house, and the August air was stifling. She went to bed and lay sweating on a thin mattress, desperate for a bit of air to cool her down. Instead, it felt as if she was lying in an oven. The team got a doctor, who diagnosed Lis with severe malaria. Her temperature rose to 105 on and off for five days. Because it wasn't easy to communicate at the time, Hans and I didn't hear about Lis having malaria until she recovered and sent a letter to us.

This impressed on me the importance of intercession for our children. I will not always know the situation they are facing, but God does. Often he will nudge me to pray for them at different times, and later I find out that they needed prayer at those specific times. Over time I developed a habit and a deep love for intercession. I would not only pray for my children, but also for the countries where they were working. It was my way to be able to get involved in what they were doing and share in their work. Sometimes God gave me words and pictures for their situations, and I was able to encourage them with those. Intercession also helps dispel worry and fear, as it is something you can practically do to give your children to God.

Like his sisters, Dan also contracted a serious illness. In 1991 he had been working with an eye clinic in Sheberghan, Afghanistan. A couple of weeks later he was back home in California on a planned break. While he was with us, he began to feel ill. At first he thought it was just the flu, so he decided to get some rest. But as the hours went by, he seemed to be getting worse and worse. We took him to the doctor, and after a blood test the doctor said that Dan had contracted hepatitis A. We guessed it must have been from contaminated water in Sheberghan.

By this point Dan's skin had turned a jaundiced yellow, and he was very weak. The doctor gasped when he saw Dan's white blood cell count, normally between 50 and 100. The worst the doctor had seen was 4,100. Dan's count was 6,200. The prognosis was not good; the doctor said we had to prepare for Dan not making it. At home we did the most important thing we could do—pray. As we did, Dan, back at home, said he felt something shift spiritually, and he knew he was going to be okay. It took six weeks, but Dan recovered fully. I was so thankful that the Lord, our Healer, was with our children wherever they went.

In addition to all the excitement and stories of victories that we shared together in Switzerland, there was also sadness. Elisabeth tearfully told us that before they left for Switzerland, their former maid, Premila, had been killed. She had been in an arranged marriage for five years. Her mother-in-law had taken a disliking to her and had plotted with her son to create an "accident." One day, as Premila was cooking in the family home, her mother-in-law poured kerosene on Premila's sari and it ignited. Premila's husband called her parents and told them to pick up their badly burned daughter. With burns on 80 percent of her body, Premila died three days later. This kind of vengeful killing happens often in India. Lis and Steve felt the death of Premila very keenly.

I was particularly saddened by the story because I remembered Premila. When we had visited Pune several years earlier, I had met her. At the time she was a beautiful seventeen-year-old girl from a village, excited and a little nervous about the arranged marriage she was going into. I grieved knowing the outcome had been so tragic. Later, Lis told us that the husband and the mother-in-law were sent to prison.

Greg and Christina were glad to be in the cooler weather of Switzerland and out of the intense heat of New Delhi, where they now lived. They had recently spent three months in Kashmir, and they shared story after story of open doors for ministry there. Greg had been teaching and training new believers how to reach out to their own people and to plant churches. One time he went with a team into a village, and they were asked to pray for a militant with a kidney disease. After they prayed, the man was completely healed. Christina met with the Kashmiri believing women. She gathered them together and encouraged them as much as she could. She urged them to meet together while she was gone, support each other, and study the Bible.

Christina and Greg now had two sons. Caleb had started a German preschool in Delhi and was learning his grandfather's mother language. Micah, born in 1998, had recently gotten the cast off his foot, which he had broken when he ran out into the street between moving cars.

Though our grandchildren lived far away, Hans and I were able to see some of them at least once a year during their visits home or our visits abroad. Our Swiss holiday was fun for the cousins to play and get to know each other better.

Later that night Hans and I reflected on the lives our children were leading. We were so proud of them. Hans often said he was a rich man because of his children, and he meant it. He was only sorry he didn't have more children to "send" to share the good news of Jesus to the world. I was humbled and privileged that God chose to use our children to bless so many. The cost of missing them, of the dangers they had been in, of not having them close by, was all worth it when I thought of the lives they had impacted with the love of Christ.

Our eight days together were over all too soon, but not before we had a big family celebration with over thirty Swiss cousins and relatives, feasting on bratwurst and potato salad outside in the sunshine while enjoying the gorgeous Swiss panorama.

GRANDCHILDREN ANNALISA, CALEB, CARIN & MICAH

It was time to say good-bye, again. The words of a song called "Give of Your Best to the Master," written by Howard B. Grose in 1902, expressed what God had done in my life and theirs:

> Give of your best to the Master, give of the strength
>   of your youth.
> Throw your soul's fresh glowing ardor, into the
>   battle for truth.
> Jesus has set the example, dauntless was He, young
>   and brave;
> Give Him your loyal devotion, give Him the best
>   that you have.

Give of your best to the Master;
Give of the strength of your youth.
Clad in Salvation's full armor;
Join in the battle for truth.

Give of your best to the Master, give Him first place
in your heart.
Give Him first place in your service, consecrate
every part.
Give, and to you will be given, God His beloved
Son gave.
Gratefully seeking to serve Him, give Him the best
that you have.

Give of your best to the Master, naught else is worthy His love.
He gave Himself for your ransom, gave up His glory
above.
Laid down His life without murmur you from sin's
ruin to save.
Give Him your heart's adoration, give Him the best
that you have.

As we waved the children off at the end of the reunion, I
felt very thankful and satisfied that Hans and I had led such
a full and wonderful life. Putting God first in our lives and in
the lives of our children had brought immeasurable rewards.
God had never let us down. In joys and hardships he proved
he was there, protecting and providing, fulfilling his promises. Releasing our children into his care and will for their

lives was the best thing we had ever done. It may not have been easy all the time, but it was worth it!

GUNILA, DAN, ELISABETH, HANS & CHRISTINA

Principles to Live By

- When our children are grown, we can look forward to helping them release their own children into God's loving purposes for the nations.

- Putting God first in our own lives and the lives of our children brings immeasurable rewards, including the blessings of seeing grandchildren (even if they live in other nations). God will never let us down.

14

HANS FINISHES HIS COURSE

For when David had served God's purpose
in his own generation, he fell asleep.
—ACTS 13:36

IN 2006 we spent a wonderful summer in Sweden with Dan, Steve, Elisabeth and their girls. Later we traveled to Switzerland to see Greg, Christina, and family, which now also included their daughter Kesia, born in 2003. While in Switzerland, Hans came down with pneumonia. After staying in the hospital for a few days, he recuperated quickly, and we traveled home to Colorado.

Over the coming months, however, Hans did not feel up to par. Now seventy-nine, he went to the doctor for a checkup in November and was diagnosed with a fast-growing leukemia. He spent four weeks in the hospital in Pueblo, Colorado, about two hours from our home. The doctor believed that Hans did not have long to live. He asked if we wanted nature to take its course, but we decided to try some treatment. Hans had four sessions of chemotherapy, but the dose could not be too heavy, because he had a congenital heart problem.

During this time in the hospital, Hans and I had peace. How wonderful it was to know that "our times are in his hands."

Elisabeth, Dan, and Christina came home to see their dad, and we celebrated a blessed Thanksgiving together in the hospital. Christina had written a beautiful tribute, which she framed and gave to him to read. You could see the pleasure and pride on Hans's face as he read his daughter's words:

Dad,

You have always demonstrated unconditional love towards me in all the seasons of my life. Your desire to follow Jesus was modeled in your life and was one that I wanted to follow. In all the decisions in my life you have been a father who pointed me to Jesus and "what would Jesus do?" This is a treasure you helped plant in my heart. Now I get to bless other people with the same desire to follow Jesus. You blessed me with boldness to go anywhere Jesus would lead. You never saw a closed door but had faith that God could lead us to any place to share the love of Jesus. I am so glad to have a father who came from Switzerland! In the last few years I have gotten to know more about Switzerland and am proud to now have not only the strengths of America but Swiss strengths as well.

You blessed me by your faithfulness to God, your family, church, and work. You never gave up! Like the great builder you are, you also "built" a family who learned how to be loyal to God and others.

You also instilled an adventurous spirit that prepared us well for missionary life. Hiking in the mountains and traveling to different parts of the world prepared us for what we are doing now.

Thank you for helping us to focus on what matters most in life. You never got caught up in material things. The memories can go on and on, how you passed on a blessing to me. This is just a small reminder for you to read of how wonderful a father you are to me! I am grateful you are my dad!

Love,

Christina

Hans put the letter down and beckoned for Christina to come close. She moved to the bed, and he kissed her cheek, his eyes glistening with tears. This was the last time they would see each other here on earth.

At Christmastime Hans was glad to be able to come home from the hospital for a few weeks. He, Dan, and I celebrated Christmas with Swiss fondue. On Wednesday, January 17, at Hans's request, we took a drive to nearby Tercio Ranch to see the herds of elk. This was the ranch that YWAM had initially planned to buy, and the prospect of owning a piece of it had drawn us to Colorado. The next day Hans got a fever for a few hours, and by Saturday he was very weak and wanted to go back to the hospital. The next day, January 21, 2007, Hans went to his reward, into his loving Savior's presence. He would have been eighty years old on March 1.

Struck with grief, I was carried through the motions, organizing the funeral and letting people know that Hans had gone home.

There was a clean blanket of snow the day my husband was laid to rest at Stonewall Cemetery. The Lord blessed us with sunshine for a few hours, and some of us walked from the church to the cemetery about a mile away. Hans wanted to be buried in a "pine box," and two friends crafted a beautiful pine casket for him.

HANS'S LAST JOURNEY

In the service Elisabeth shared some beautiful words in memory of her father:

My dad was mission-minded. He was very youthful and loved young people. He was faithful to God, his wife, kids, church, his work, and his word. Dad was artistic and built a beautiful cabin. He had the big perspective and believed the impossible was possible with God. He had a great sense of humor and would joke and tease all the time. He was an encourager. He inspired and challenged us to be radical. He was a risk taker.

Dad was a selfless person—giving and reaching out to others in need. Always a hard worker, he was very active and full of energy. He was a great story-teller with a great memory, and he trusted God with us as we went to different parts of the world.

Later, Dan reflected on his father:

There isn't a day that goes by when I don't miss my dad. It is hard to describe in words how blessed I was. He was consistent his whole life, like a steady rock. He never wavered in his faith or values. His faith in Jesus was the rudder that steered his life. He was always pushing me towards God and his will for my life. He trusted me and released me to do what was in my heart, even if it meant moving to the other side of the world. My dad had a great sense of humor; it was very dry and wonderfully refreshing. He was always ready to lighten the mood and help people feel relaxed. He was quick to humble himself and make things right before the day was over. My dad was great at making new friends. He was excellent at his trade—and quite stubborn in a good way.

His fortitude and relentless commitment to God has been an amazing model for me. My dad always wanted the best for us. I can hear him saying, "Just do what God tells you."

In old-fashioned Swiss tradition, the casket was carried by horse and carriage from church to its resting place. We sang "Amazing Grace" as a last farewell. Hans had truly served God's purpose in his own generation!

GUNILA AND HANS, JERUSALEM, 1999

Hans and I would not celebrate our fiftieth anniversary together. But I wondered if that was why our children had blessed us abundantly on our fortieth anniversary. That year, without our knowledge, they had contacted friends and relatives around the world, asking if they would join in a financial blessing for us. The children felt we had helped and blessed them so much through the years, and they wanted to do something special for us in return. Through the generosity of many people, we were able to take a trip to Israel, which had been Hans's longtime dream. We saw many biblical sites and attended the Feast of Tabernacles in Jerusalem. On our way home we visited Sweden. We were truly humbled as our children rose up to call us blessed.

Principles to Live By

- "Just do what God tells you" are some of the greatest words parents can say to their children.

- As we trust God with our children's lives, they in time will rise up and call us blessed.

15

TURNING THE CORNER

Her children arise and call her blessed.
—PROVERBS 31:28

AFTER HANS died, I entered a difficult period of grief and adjustment. I leaned on the support of my children and friends and, above all, my Lord. In March 2007 I went with Dan to YWAM in Montana, where he was teaching on "Passion for God" in the Discipleship Training School. I was so impressed by the gift God had given him to speak and challenge young people to know God more and serve him in missions.

A few months later, in June, I went to Chico, California, to an In Touch gathering of former YWAMers and friends of YWAM. Peter and Donna Jordan, the leaders of In Touch, became dear and special friends to me. Donna encouraged me with these words from the Lord: "Trust me. Rely on me and my love. I will lead you and guide you. It's a day of new beginnings."

During a quiet time at the gathering, the Lord spoke directly to me: "Come away, my beloved. I'll love you and teach you my ways. I have great deposits in you that need to be drawn out. Ride with me, and I'll drive. Keep being yielded to me. I'll take you to the right destination. Don't be afraid to go alone." As I continued to pray, God spoke from Psalm 78: "We will tell the next generation the praiseworthy deeds of the LORD, his power, and the wonders he has done" (v. 4). I had an inkling then that God was asking me to write a book about my life and experiences.

In July I took a trip to Kona, Hawaii, where Dan was now based. We had a blessed time together. He took me to the Coffee Shack, my favorite breakfast place, where I ordered papaya and eggs. We also went hiking and fishing with our friends Andy and Susan Huddleston. Dan caught a large Ono (a favorite Hawaiian fish), which Andy barbequed for a delicious meal. I was being refreshed spiritually and physically in Kona.

God encouraged me through the speakers at the community meetings at the University of the Nations. John Dawson said something that stood out to me: "What are you asking God for? God is the biggest dreamer." And Darlene Cunningham said, "God has prepared you for such a time as this. Do whatever he tells you!"

I also joined the writers' group on the University of the Nations (U of N) campus. I had the opportunity to listen to Enid Scratch (Darlene Cunningham's mother) reading from the story she was writing about her life. Was I to do the same? The faint nudge from the Lord to write my book was getting louder. "Lord, help me get going," was my prayer.

The Lord put in my heart that I was to come back to Kona and serve in a practical way as a Mission Builder on the YWAM campus. But first I would take another trip to India and Nepal.

In October 2007 YWAM Nepal was celebrating its twenty-fifth anniversary. Elisabeth and Steve were going to be there and asked me to come along. I traveled to Pune, India, to meet them and enjoy spending time with their family. While there, I read a book about Walt Disney. He said, "Don't waste your experiences—let them inspire you. Dream bold dreams. Don't fear failure but learn the lesson and try again. Never do less than your best." Again, the Lord was encouraging me to move on with him and get going on the book.

In Nepal the Lord showed me that part of my inheritance were the Nepalese people who were now seeking God because of the witness of my children. I had let my daughter go to Nepal twenty-five years earlier to start a work, and now three to four hundred workers and children were gathered to celebrate God's faithfulness in a compound outside Kathmandu. My heart was overflowing with gratefulness to my wonderful Lord who let me be part of the harvest in his kingdom. I can only imagine what eternity will be like when we receive our full inheritances!

After my time with Elisabeth and Steve, I was grateful to stay with Greg and Christina in Delhi for a few weeks. They were busy training church planters and leading Bible studies and house meetings. We all enjoyed great fellowship at the International Church. Caleb and Micah were attending the German school and played baseball at the American embassy. It was so fun to experience life with them all. They also comforted me when the pain of losing Hans hit me, causing my eyes to well up with tears of grief and sudden loneliness.

This grieving came in waves. I no longer had Hans to share my feelings and thoughts with or to cuddle up with. I could no longer feel his tender strokes on my cheek or look into his eyes and have understanding between us without any need for words. But how wonderful it was to be able to take everything to God in prayer! He was there in my grieving—waiting, listening, understanding, comforting. He never left me.

I returned to Kona to serve as a Mission Builder in the library at the U of N in 2008. I realized that the Lord was helping me find my own new identity. For most of my life I had lived for my husband and my children. I had moved from my childhood home right into marriage, and now I was, for the first time, out on my own. I fasted and prayed, seeking the Lord for direction in my life. I wanted to draw closer to Jesus and hear his voice clearer. The Lord spoke through Psalm 25:12–14. He said that he will instruct me in the way chosen for me; I will spend my days in prosperity, and my descendants will inherit the land; he will confide in me and make his covenant known to me—as I fear him. Thank you, Jesus!

He also gave me inspiration and direction regarding the writing of my book. Peter writes, "With the help of Silas, whom I regard as a faithful brother, I have written to you briefly, encouraging you and testifying that this is the true grace of God. Stand fast in it" (1 Pet. 5:12). I realized that I didn't have to write my book alone. "Lord, who is my 'Silas'?" I asked.

A few months later in Kona, I met Jemimah Wright, a freelance writer. With her help this project got started. She was one of God's wonderful provisions and blessings—my "Silas."

While my writing project got under way, I was also praying for my house in Colorado to sell. The Lord answered my prayers, providing a good buyer even in a falling housing market. Steve and Elisabeth and girls had decided to move to the United States for a time so that the girls could go to high school here. They invited me to come and live with them in Gig Harbor, Washington, where they moved to be near Steve's parents and their very supportive church. This was a special blessing for me.

Another blessing came when Christina and Greg surprised me with another grandchild. Joshua was born September 29, 2008, and I traveled back to India to welcome mother and baby home to their flat in Delhi. What joy to spend another three weeks with my children and grandchildren in Delhi!

At the end of the year, I was back in Kona. I again enjoyed my papaya and egg breakfast at the Coffee Shack. This time I had been invited by Peter and Donna Jordan to staff the All Nations All Generations DTS. Students ages sixteen to seventy-six came from many nations. This was a time of stretching and learning for me. I was feeling my inadequacy, lack of confidence, and inability to take initiative. It was a big school with over seventy students, a full schedule, and many new names to remember. Leaders and staff were patient with me, encouraging and helping me along the way. It was so rewarding to see many lives changed and challenged to love and serve God.

The Lord ministered greatly to me through the wonderful teachings we heard. A longtime dream of mine to go to China was realized when I helped lead an outreach team from the school there. My spirit especially thrived as we prayed along the North Korean border and worked with ministries with an emphasis on North Korea.

VISITING GRANDCHILDREN IN NEW DELHI, 2008

I returned home at the end of May 2009 and moved in with Steve and Elisabeth in Gig Harbor. The transition was hard in many ways. I felt very alone making such a big move without Hans. I took one step at a time, being led by the Lord. I didn't feel ready to put down deep roots in a new place.

In August my niece was getting married in Sweden, and I rejoiced to go and be part of the wedding. My friend Rose-Marie and I were both turning seventy in September, a week apart. So a visit with her, eating her mocha meringue cake, was a special treat. She surprised me with a sixth grade school reunion that she had organized. Eight of us—some of the girls who heard us play and sing about Jesus many years ago—met and reminisced in Falkenberg, where I grew up.

I also went to Switzerland to see Lotti, Hans's sister. With the remaining money in Hans and my Swiss bank account, I treated Lotti to breakfast at the Dolder, a five-star hotel in Zurich. Hans wanted to have breakfast there the last time we were in Switzerland, but it was being remodeled. I felt him smiling on us from heaven.

It is now three years after Hans died, and I have turned a corner. Just as Jesus rose three days after his death, I feel new resurrection life three years after Hans's death. Jesus has comforted me and is drawing me to himself. I love him! My children have also been wonderful to encourage and care for me and welcome me into their homes.

Today I am accepting joyfully where I am in life, walking tenderly with my God, listening to his voice, and being content. Like Brother Lawrence, the author of *The Practice of the Presence of God,* I am more aware of God's presence daily, finding constant pleasure in his divine company, speaking with him in all seasons. As Paul said, "I press on to take hold of that for which Christ took hold of me" (Phil. 3:12). I am humbly grateful that all my children and grandchildren love, follow, and serve the Lord. May the nations and peoples be blessed as they—and I—continue to faithfully love God and love people.

Principles to Live By

- God gives us as a spiritual inheritance the very people our children have poured their lives into.

- In whatever twists and turns our lives and our children's lives take, we can joyfully accept where we are (and they are) in contentment, continuing to let go of control and trusting in God's loving leadership.

- God will never leave us alone over our lifetime on earth. He will never forget our needs and the needs of our children.

Epilogue

It is springtime in Gig Harbor, Washington. The other day I was driving to pick up Carin, my oldest granddaughter, from her friend's house. The fruit trees and rhododendrons were in bloom, the birch trees just sprouting new green leaves. The afternoon sun made the landscape delightful to my senses. A feeling of contentment and peace came over me. The Lord has done great things in my life and in the lives of each member of my family.

My children are all thriving where they have been placed. Elisabeth and Steve, now based in the United States for a season, are still deeply involved with YWAM in South Asia and the Muslim world. Currently Elisabeth is heading the campaign for Pure Hope Pakistan, to raise money for one hundred thousand water filters in response to the recent flooding in the country that affected twenty million people. She also speaks in churches and teaches in YWAM schools. Steve continues to teach and speak at YWAM conferences and schools and in university settings. He advises mission leaders and is finishing his PhD through the Oxford Centre for Mission Studies in England. My granddaughters are now in their junior and sophomore years of high school.

Dan is traveling to teach in YWAM bases around the world. He was recently in Nigeria, where hundreds of militants came to know the Lord. Over one hundred have done a DTS in the country and have joined YWAM to be missionaries to their people. One of the men Dan spent time with was named Nature. This man had been a militant leader and involved in all sorts of evil, including burying people alive. Nature had an encounter with Jesus and is now working with YWAM with a vision to see his nation reached for Christ.

Christina and Greg and their four children are still serving with YWAM in India, pioneering evangelism and church planting among the Muslims in the north. Their vision is to accelerate the spread of the gospel to Muslims. Greg spends much of his time networking, teaching, and training believers as well as encouraging church-planting movements. Most of Christina's time is spent homeschooling their four children in New Delhi.

And me. I do miss Hans, but my Lord's friendship and companionship grows sweeter and dearer, and I know He is always with me. Where I once sent out my own children to missions, I am now part of sending out spiritual "children" in the All Nations All Generations DTS in Kona. My heart is full of praise for what God has done in my life and in the lives of all my children.

I join with King David in Psalm 16:5–6:

LORD, you have assigned me my portion and my cup;
 you have made my lot secure.
The boundary lines have fallen for me in pleasant places;
 surely I have a delightful inheritance.

Appendix A: Additional Reflections on Releasing Children

*Here am I, and the children the LORD has given me. We
are signs and symbols . . . from the LORD Almighty.*
—ISAIAH 8:18

Over the years I have learned many lessons about releasing
my children into God's purposes for them. I hope what I have
learned will encourage and help parents who are in similar
circumstances.

Release

Letting my children go has come out of my love, devo-
tion, and intimacy with the Lord. As I learned to know the
Lord more and to understand his love for people who have
never heard about him, I wanted to be part of his desire and
intent for all people to hear the good news.

Release is an important part of this. It was when the boy
with the bread and fishes (John 6) released what he had that
God used it and multiplied it by thousands. When Hannah
released her son Samuel to the Lord and his service (1 Samuel
1), God used Samuel's life mightily to lead a nation.

I am so grateful that my children have wanted to spread
the gospel. They have learned to trust God to speak to them,
lead them, and care for them. He loves them more than I do,
and he has given me abundant joy. He has greatly rewarded
me according to his promise: "No one who has left home or

brothers or sisters or mother or father or *children* or fields for me and the gospel will fail to receive a *hundred times* as much in this present age (homes, brothers, sisters, mothers, *children* and fields—and with them, persecutions) and in the age to come, eternal life" (Mark 10:29–30, emphasis added).

Prayer and Reading the Word

Prayer is a must. It is where I can cast worries, fears, disappointments, and questions on Jesus—while praising and worshiping him. Prayer, together with reading the Word, is the place to get peace, instruction, and understanding as one takes time to listen to the Lord. "Come near to God and he will come near to you" (James 4:8). This is where I have learned about God's character, how to trust him, and how to be a better mother.

Parenting

Parenting is the most influential job in the world. So relax, don't compare, be available, learn to listen, be consistent, and encourage. Be a good example—in speaking, giving, praying, reading God's Word, and trusting God for provision. The safest place for our children to be—wherever they are in the world—is in obedience to God's will for their lives. Though the circumstances and outcomes may be different from what we want, we must remember that God loves our children and is sovereign.

I relinquish the right to control my children to God, who knows what is best for them. Of course, I was very concerned for Elisabeth and Dan when they were in prison for the gospel's sake. Confidence came by praying, recognizing God's character, receiving comfort from the Word, and knowing that, whatever happened, my children had been obedient to the next thing God had called them to do. God was fulfilling his purposes. I had to choose not to worry but to trust and pray. "Do not be anxious about anything, but in everything, by prayer and petition, with thanksgiving, present your requests to God. And the peace of God which transcends all understanding, will guard your hearts and minds in Christ Jesus" (Phil. 4:6–7).

Fear

I am glad my children wanted to be risk-takers. At times when they were scared to launch out, I said to them, "Obey God more than men, and use wisdom." Our command is to go into *all the world* and make disciples. That includes not just places that seem safe but also war zones and areas of persecution.

When Dan was in prison in Iran, I didn't know in the beginning if he was dead or alive. During panicky moments, I would quote scriptures, reflect on God's character in my mind, and pray. Many times, instead of fear, I have experienced the peace of God that passes understanding (Phil. 4:7). Isaiah 26:3 says, "You will keep in perfect peace him whose mind is steadfast, because he trusts in you."

Our promise is that "perfect love drives out fear" (1 John 4:18), and in Jesus' name we can resist the spirit of fear. Fear tried to grip me when I heard through the media that the American embassy near Dan in Beirut had been bombed. I chose to pray, trusting in God's promises. Knowing that Dan was where the Lord wanted him helped to bring peace.

Reputation

As a young girl I learned that following Jesus is not always popular with your peers. When I was ridiculed, I found great joy, and nothing others did would change my choice to walk with my Master. When it looked crazy to others that all our children were missionaries, we were excited that our children had chosen what was best for their lives instead of settling for just good.

Education

Education is the process of training and developing knowledge, skills, and character. Where better to get this grounding than in a Christian setting? Our children were learning God's Word while learning to love and follow the Lord, pray and seek his guidance, depend on him for finances and support, and work in teams. They also learned about new people and cultures, world geography, and leadership skills.

Some of my children's education came through coursework, and some came through life experiences in uncommon learning settings. This might not be the American ideal, but God has a bigger, more global plan for his children. I am glad that Dan pursued his college degree, because he obeyed the Lord, and his degree helped him get into Afghanistan, where God was leading him. Often in our society, the purpose of educational pursuit is for a financially secure future in an enjoyable career, and success means attaining wealth, position, and honor. But in God's kingdom we walk to a different drumbeat. Success is obedience to the Lord, and he is our security, our provider, our wisdom, our fulfillment and joy in life.

Finances and Giving

It's been a walk together with our children to learn to trust the Lord who promises that he "will meet all [our] needs according to his glorious riches in Christ Jesus" (Phil. 4:19). It starts with giving: "Give, and it will be given to you" (Luke 6:38). I still remember the great joy I felt as I walked to the post office with a check to help Elisabeth in an early YWAM school. Our account was almost down to zero, and we were putting our trust in God's faithfulness to provide for our needs as well as our children's. Now, after about thirty years, I can say that God continues to be totally faithful. He has supplied all our needs—for the children and us—and all of us are greatly blessed.

It has been tight at times, and finances sometimes came at the last minute. God has tested us to see if we would trust him as our provider, and in response he has done wonderful miracles. God provided a loan so that we could remodel our home and pay for Dan's college tuition in the perfect "last minute." When Dan graduated, he was able to go right away to serve the Lord on foreign soil.

Giving is a heart matter, and I pray for people and churches to be touched to partner in the Lord's work and support children and youth. I live by the motto "But seek first his kingdom and his righteousness, and all these things [food, clothes, shelter, and treasures] will be given to you as well" (Matt. 6:33). Jesus also said, "Store up for yourselves treasures in heaven. . . . For where your treasure is, there your heart will be also" (Matt. 6:20–21).

Health and Sickness

It is not easy to hear that your child is sick while on the other side of the world. Living in Asia made my children more susceptible to illnesses like dysentery, amoebas, fever, and diarrhea (especially in the beginning). They have also had other diseases like malaria, typhoid, and hepatitis. I am glad they had access to doctors and medicine that was inexpensive. We were relieved, however, that Dan did not need to go to the hospital for his hepatitis, because he had no health insurance at the time. It's amazing how the Lord looks out for the details in every moment as we pray and commit our lives to him.

It seems all the children were challenged physically before venturing into a new assignment from the Lord. Elisabeth developed an ovarian cyst before moving to Nepal, but it ruptured without an operation, and she was restored. Dan had a broken elbow as he launched out to study at Wheaton, and the school took care of his medical bill. Christina had a kidney infection as she started the School of Biblical Studies in Hong Kong, and God supplied for her medical bill. She has had some other surgeries while living in India, and medical insurance covered the cost of her surgeries and treatment. It is awesome to see how God has provided in each situation. Even when Elisabeth had malaria in Calcutta, God provided wonderful Christian workers who cared for her and got her help from the governor's doctor.

In these many health situations I have had to learn to cast my burdens on the Lord, knowing that he, the Lord and Healer, cares for my children.

Communication

It has been vital for me to hear my children's hearts through letters, cards, e-mails, faxes, and telephone calls. Communicating and knowing how they are doing has greatly helped me release them. Though I could not always help provide their needs, it was important to know how to pray and wonderful to hear and share their praise reports. My availability also helped them to have someone to contact quickly, like when they lost a passport or credit card, needed particular information, or wanted to know the amount in their bank accounts. I functioned as their banker and sometimes helped to get funds to them.

Visits

Our travels have been worth every penny! Beginning with our first trip to Hawaii to visit Elisabeth, Hans or I or both of us have seen our children in many parts of the world. We went to Nepal after Elisabeth was released from prison, and we helped out in Afghanistan for ten weeks when Dan was there. We traveled to India several times. It has helped to know about our children's situations, to meet their friends, experience the same hard beds and stomach problems, worship with native believers, and see the fruit of the children's labor for the Lord. Between our traveling and their traveling, we have usually seen each other at least once a year.

Grandchildren

When I hear others talking about their grandchildren, I thank the Lord for the special grace he has given me. I have lived far away from my grandchildren and have not seen them grow up. Though I have missed them, it has not been too difficult to handle. I was able to see all of them soon after they were born, sometimes at home in the United States and sometimes in other countries. I have been blessed by the time I have spent with my children and grandchildren—wherever they have been.

Appendix B: On Prayer

Devote yourselves to prayer, being watchful and thankful.
—COLOSSIANS 4:2

Prayer and hearing from the Lord have been essential in letting my children go. If you don't know the One your children are serving and working for, I pray you seek him now. May you receive his love, forgiveness, peace, joy, and lordship—you just need to ask him for it. It will transform you, and you will learn to love the things he loves.

Prayer is a relationship, a friendship with God. Prayer is mankind's way to know God intimately. It is the very breath of spiritual life. It is the human soul on its knees.

"Man does not live on bread alone, but on every word that comes from the mouth of God" (Matt. 4:4). Hearing the Father's voice is life to our souls. One way of hearing from God is through the Scriptures. The Word of God has guided my life and has revealed Jesus Christ to me. Reading the Word of God and praying go hand in hand. Often I am reminded of a scripture, and I will say it back to God, agreeing with the truth.

Although there is no one formula for prayer, I like to start my prayer time with praise and adoration to my Lord. Here the Psalms can be a great help. In Psalm 96:2–10 we read:

Sing to the LORD, praise his name;
    proclaim his salvation day after day.

Declare his glory among the nations. . . .
For great is the LORD and most worthy of praise;
    he is to be feared above all gods. . . .
Splendor and majesty are before him;
    strength and glory are in his sanctuary. . . .
Worship the LORD in the splendor of His
    holiness. . . .
Say among the nations, "The LORD reigns."

Giving my children back to the Lord in prayer, acknowledging they are his, helped me release them. Prayer helped my heart not to hold on too tightly. God's Spirit helped my spirit to do like Hannah, who said, "I prayed for this child, and the LORD has granted me what I asked of him. So now I give him to the LORD" (1 Sam. 1:27–28). Hannah then brought clothes to her son, caring for him where he served the Lord away from home (2:19). This has been my part also.

This is just a sample of how the Lord and I have communicated, talking back and forth during prayer times. To him be the glory for wisdom, peace, guidance, and support—to help me let my (his) children go!

Appendix C:
To Mothers of Missionaries

Words attributed to Winona Carroll,
missionary to India

So send I you—to give your own with gladness,
To let them go unhindered to the lost.
To hide the tears and every trace of sadness,
So send I you—to taste with Me the cost.

So send I you—to anxious days of waiting
For word that often leaves so much untold.
To nights of burdened vigil unabating,
So send I you—to watch the gap you hold.

So send I you—to walk alone when aged,
To need the strength of one you cannot call.
To lean on Me and on the ones I bring you,
So send I you—to find in Me your all.

So send I you—to know the joy of serving,
To share the triumphs of the one you send,
To reap the fruit of sacrifice unswerving.
So send I you—to joy without an end.

As the Father has sent Me, so send I you.

About the Authors

GUNILA BAUMANN was born in Sweden and moved to the United States at age fourteen. She and her late husband Hans, born in Switzerland, raised their three children in Southern California, teaching them to love God and love people. Each of her children has worked with Youth With A Mission (YWAM) for over twenty years in different parts of the world, and two of them have been imprisoned for the gospel's sake. Gunila has been a homemaker, loves to pray for people around the globe and entertain missionaries, and has been involved with short-term missions in Asia and Europe. She now lives in Kona, Hawaii, and works with Discipleship Training Schools at YWAM's University of the Nations.

JEMIMAH WRIGHT is a freelance journalist working for the national press in England. She studied at Oxford Brookes University, spent a year in Cape Town helping children affected by AIDS, and then returned to England to train as a journalist. Jemimah has written several books for YWAM Publishing, including *Taking the High Places* and *A Way Beyond Death*. She is based in London, England. To contact her, e-mail jemimah@wrightfeatures.co.uk.